Burning Down the House

Other Books by Charles Baxter

NOVELS

First Light
Shadow Play
The Feast of Love
Saul and Patsy
The Soul Thief

SHORT STORIES

Harmony of the World
Through the Safety Net
A Relative Stranger
Believers

POETRY

Imaginary Paintings

NONFICTION

The Art of Subtext: Beyond Plot

EDITOR

*The Business of Memory: The Art of Remembering
    in an Age of Forgetting*
*Bringing the Devil to His Knees: The Craft of Fiction
    and the Writing Life* (with Peter Turchi)
Best New American Voices 2001
A William Maxwell Portrait
    (with Michael Collier and Edward Hirsch)
The Art of series

Burning Down the House

Essays on Fiction

Second, Expanded Edition

CHARLES BAXTER

Graywolf Press

Publication of this volume is made possible in part by a grant provided by the Minnesota State Arts Board, through an appropriation by the Minnesota State Legislature; a grant from the Wells Fargo Foundation Minnesota; and a grant from the National Endowment for the Arts, which believes that a great nation deserves great art. Significant support has also been provided by the Bush Foundation; Target; the McKnight Foundation; and other generous contributions from foundations, corporations, and individuals. To these organizations and individuals we offer our heartfelt thanks.

Published by Graywolf Press
212 Third Avenue North, Suite 485
Minneapolis, Minnesota 55401
All rights reserved.

www.graywolfpress.org

Published in the United States of America

ISBN 978-1-55597-508-1

8   10   12   14   13   11   9   7

Library of Congress Control Number: 2008928248

Cover design: Scott Sorenson

Cover art: *Staircase, Doylestown* by Charles Sheeler. Hirshhorn Museum and Sculpture Garden, Smithsonian Institution, Gift of the Joseph H. Hirshhorn Foundation, 1972. Photographer: Lee Stalsworth.

Acknowledgments

Among those I wish to thank for help and support are my colleagues in the University of Michigan MFA program, especially Nicholas Delbanco, along with the other members of the Department of English. My students have been a constant source of stimulus and help to me. My great debt in these essays is to the members of the Program for Writers at Warren Wilson College, both students and faculty. These essays are dedicated to the founder of that program, Ellen Bryant Voigt.

My thanks to the editors of the magazines and journals in which some of these essays first appeared: "The Donald Barthelme Blues" and "Fiction and the Inner Life of Objects" in the *Gettysburg Review;* "Stillness" in *DoubleTake;* "Counterpointed Characterization" in *AWP Chronicle;* "Dysfunctional Narratives, or 'Mistakes Were Made'" in *Ploughshares;* "Rhyming Action" in *Michigan Quarterly Review;* "Against Epiphanies" in *jacaranda;* "Sonya's Last Speech, or, Double Voicing" in *Colorado Review;* and "Regarding Happiness" in the *Southern Review.*

Thanks also to the Lila Wallace-Reader's Digest Foundation and to the University of Michigan for support during the time when these essays were written.

Contents

FOR
Ellen Bryant Voigt

Preface to the
Second Edition

Looking over these essays several years after they were first published, I am struck by the nerve—the sheer gall, as people used to say—of the guy who wrote them. I am no longer that particular guy, but I still have to be answerable to what he said. In a way, these essays have followed me around, and I *have* had to answer for them. At the time, I thought I was writing a book of literary criticism with a few glances at the culture at large. A harmless project, or so I thought. How could literary criticism, a drab enterprise, possibly annoy anybody?

But in the years since the book first came out, I have been asked angrily—several times—in the Q & A sessions following my readings, "Why are you against epiphanies?" I was called by a reporter for a famous newspaper who wanted to know whether I thought President Bill Clinton was guilty of concocting a *dysfunctional narrative* during the Monica Lewinsky scandal (he was, but all the other presidents of our benighted time have disavowed their responsibility for bad outcomes by using the "mistakes were made" weaselism). Readers have let me know that I have been weak-minded and a deliberate obfuscator. Some poets' noses have been put out of joint by what I said about their behavior in "Rhyming Action." My college English teacher took the time to write to me to say that he didn't like my views on objects.

For the record, not that it matters greatly, I think epiphanies are infinitely precious, and the genuine ones unimaginably rare. I think dysfunctional narratives have become a plague on our society; stillness is a more uncommon condition than ever; melodrama remains a largely unconsidered category; anthropomorphized objects still go unnoticed; and Donald Barthelme is an underrated writer (or overrated for the wrong reasons). And criticism can still wake people up.

The reactions I've had to this book show what can happen if a critic tries to make some connections between the culture's way of telling stories to itself and the literary texts that people in the culture actually read. I didn't want to write a how-to book. I *did* want to put together a book that might get readers upset and excited, and that might point out some possible paths for would-be writers to follow. In that, I may have succeeded. To my surprise, I have received quite a number of complimentary letters. The book has been assigned to classes at colleges and universities. A lady called me a few days ago from Florida to thank me. One grateful reader of this book even bought me a drink. You never know.

And, after all, we are still in Iraq, and no one is clear about why we went there in the first place, or who is responsible for those initial mistakes. Mistakes are still being made.

The two new essays in this collection were written after a group that I collected together for a short book on subtexts, also published by Graywolf, entitled *Beyond Plot*. The new ones included in this book, "Sonya's Last Speech" and "Regarding Happiness," deal with the problem of representing despair and happiness in a dramatic medium. Happiness is not a problem for anyone experiencing it, but it certainly does present a problem for a writer who wishes to dramatize it at length. Despair, in our post 9/11 world, presents us with issues equally as large—we can learn a great deal from the way that Anton Chekhov treated it.

I do hope this book will continue to get its readers involved, excited, or enraged. With any luck, the house is *still* burning.

Preface

Burning Down the House addresses a set of subjects of urgent concern to me, issues that in the broadest sense have to do with the imagination's grip on daily life and how one lives in the pressure of that grip. The essays return to the scene of writing as a location where some of these matters can be addressed, and where the pressure is greatest. Most of the essays do their best to visit the interesting wayward locales where our public lives and our private imaginings intersect: funeral homes, sites of chemical spills, summer backyard parties, press conferences. Looking them over, I find that the essays have a quality of slightly comic desperation, as if the house of the imagination had to be burned down in order for its contents to be revealed and its foundations made visible. Of course the house, as a product of the imagination, continues to stand.

We often pretend, these days, that public lying by politicians has no effect on the stories we tell each other, but it does; or that our obsession with data processing has no relevance to violence in movies, but it might. In almost every essay in this book I have tried to set forth a widespread belief or practice—the belief in Hell, for example, or the recent mania for happy endings and insight—as a precondition to the way in which storytellers (and that means almost all of us) come up with narratives and then tell them. Most of the topics arose from questions that seemed to me both social and literary, both obvious and in some sense unanswerable: Why have we come to think that most of our important memories must be traumatic? What has happened, in this century, to the way in which we think about inanimate objects?

I had hoped that by taking on some of these huge subjects, these contemporary patterns of thought, I could say something about what might be called *the storytelling of everyday life*. The habit of narrative is unceasing. We understand our lives, or try to, by the stories we tell.

These essays, as a result, are hybrid or perhaps mongrel literary productions. They are not academic essays, nor are they how-to guides; they are not even appreciations or readings of texts. Each one of them was originally written as a lecture for the MFA Program for Writers at Warren Wilson College—most of them have been substantially rewritten—but my intention was never to give any kind of direct advice. I hoped the talks would stimulate the listener to think about a social and literary matter in a way that would be naggingly helpful. I hoped, as I think most critics hope, to stimulate the audience—to provide, as Donald Barthelme once called it, "unhealthy mental excitement."

The reader may notice that one of the means I employed to create such excitement was the wild claim. There are a number of wild claims here, an occasional manic swing toward the large statement. Most of them are meant to be playful rather than ponderous, but they were intended to set fire to the house. Gertrude Stein talks about "the excitement of unsubstantiated generalities." Yes, exactly. She herself was a great creator of such generalities: *There is always something strange about the children of French notaries. . . . Americans are more interested in you than in the work you have done but they would not be interested in you at all if you had not done the work you have done.* Etc.

The topics for these excursions arose from questions or discussions that my students and friends have shared with me. Sometimes they simply arose from the headlines. The counterpointed characterization essay began with a question that my friend Miles Harvey asked me during a class break. The question was, "Whatever happened to the antagonist? There are no antagonists in the stories we write." The stillness essay grew out of my fascination with data-nausea, and it was inspired by a single phrase from James Agee that had stuck in my mind for years: "expressive air-pockets of dead silence." The melodrama essay developed from my puzzled interest in the revival, if you could call it that, of Satan and of Hell.

The incendiary and cataclysmic titles for these essays arrived on the mental scene, as such things sometimes do, while I was driving and listening to the radio. In the midst of a thirty-minute set of songs, Talking Heads' "Burning Down the House" came on. The car's right front speaker wasn't working, so that David Byrne's vehemently blank singing was virtually unaccompanied, except by an audio-fuzz background.

Something about the song—its title, its flashes of hot-and-cold abstractedness, its ability to sound like an anthem and like nonsense at the same time—keeps it close to the surfaces of memory. In the words of the novelist and critic Fred Pfeil, the pleasures announced by "Burning Down the House" will be "the bliss of escaping from codification and definition altogether, by dispersing and scattering oneself through the codes. . . ."

In these essays I wanted to escape from the definitions without necessarily creating new ones. Setting fire to something can sometimes be a wonderfully creative act, provided that the fire continues to burn.

Dysfunctional Narratives:
or: "Mistakes Were Made"

Here are some sentences of distinctive American prose from our era:

> From a combination of hypersensitivity and a desire not to know the truth in case it turned out to be unpleasant, I had spent the last ten months putting off a confrontation with John Mitchell. . . . I listened to more tapes. . . . I heard Haldeman tell me that Dean and Mitchell had come up with a plan to handle the problem of the investigation's going into areas we didn't want it to go. The plan was to call in Helms and Walters of the CIA and have them restrain the FBI. . . . Haldeman and I discussed [on the "smoking gun" tape] having the CIA limit the FBI investigation for political rather than the national security reasons I had given in my public statements. . . . On June 13, while I was in Egypt, Fred Buzhardt had suffered a heart attack. Once I was assured that he was going to pull through, I tried to assess the impact his illness would have on our legal situation.

These sentences are almost enough to make one nostalgic for an adversary with a claim upon our attention. There he is, the lawyer-president setting forth the brief for the defense, practicing the dogged art of the disclaimer in *RN: The Memoirs of Richard Nixon*. I've done some cut-and-pasting, but the sentences I've quoted are the sentences he wrote. And what sentences! Leaden and dulling, juridical-minded to the last, impersonal but not without savor—the hapless Buzhardt and his heart attack factored into the "legal situation," and that wonderful "hypersensitivity" combined with a desire "not to know the truth" that makes one think of Henry James's Lambert Strether or an epicene character in Huysmans—they present the reader with camouflage masked as objective thought.

The author of the memoir does not admit that he lied, exactly, or that he betrayed his oath of office. In his "public statements," he did a bit of false accounting, that was all. One should expect this, he suggests, from heads of state.

Indeed, the only surprise this reader had, trudging gamely through *RN* looking for clues to a badly defined mystery, was the author's report of a sentence uttered by Jacqueline Kennedy. Touring the White House after RN's election, she said, "I always live in a dream world." Funny that she would say so; funny that he would notice, and remember.

Lately I've been possessed of a singularly unhappy idea: The greatest influence on American fiction for the last twenty years may have been the author of *RN*, not in the writing but in the public character. He is the inventor, for our purposes and for our time, of the concept of *deniability*. Deniability is the almost complete disavowal of intention in relation to bad consequences. A made-up word, it reeks of the landfill-scented landscape of lawyers and litigation and high school. Following Richard Nixon in influence on recent fiction would be two runners-up, Ronald Reagan and George Bush. Their administrations put the passive voice, politically, on the rhetorical map. In their efforts to attain deniability on the arms-for-hostages deal with Iran, their administrations managed to achieve considerable notoriety for self-righteousness, public befuddlement about facts, forgetfulness under oath, and constant disavowals of political error and criminality, culminating in the quasi-confessional passive-voice-mode sentence, "Mistakes were made."

Contrast this with Robert E. Lee's statement the third day after the battle of Gettysburg and the calamity of Pickett's Charge: "All this has been my fault," Lee said. "I asked more of men than should have been asked of them."

Lee's sentences have a slightly antique ring. People just don't say such things anymore.

What difference does it make to writers of stories if public figures are denying their responsibility for their own actions? So what if they are, in effect, refusing to tell their own stories accurately? So what if the President of the United States is making himself out to be, of all things, a *victim*? Well, to make an obvious point, they create a climate in which social narratives are designed to be deliberately incoherent and misleading. Such narratives humiliate the act of storytelling. You can argue that only a coherent narrative can manage to explain public events, and you can reconstruct a story if someone says, "I made a mistake," or "We did that." You can't reconstruct a story—you can't even know what the story *is*—if everyone is saying, "Mistakes were made." Who made them? Everybody made them and no one did, and it's history anyway, so let's forget about it. Every story is a history, however, and when there is no comprehensible story, there is no history. The past, under these circumstances, becomes an unreadable mess. When we hear words like "deniability," we are in the presence of narrative dysfunction, a phrase employed by the poet C. K. Williams to describe the process by which we lose track of the story of ourselves, the story that tells us who we are supposed to be and how we are supposed to act.

The spiritual godfather of the contemporary disavowal movement, the author of *RN*, set the tenor for the times and reflected the times as well in his lifelong denial of responsibility for the Watergate break-in and cover-up. He has claimed that misjudgments were made, although not necessarily by him. Mistakes were made, although they were by no means his own, and the crimes that were committed were only crimes if you define "crime" in a certain way, in the way, for example, that his enemies like to define the word, in a manner that would be unfavorable to him, that would give him, to use a word derived from the Latin, some culpability. It wasn't the law, he claimed. It was all just politics.

A curious parallel: The Kennedy assassination may be *the* narratively dysfunctional event of our era. No one really knows who's responsible for it. One of the signs of a dysfunctional narrative is that we cannot leave it behind, and we cannot put it to rest, because it does not, finally, give us the explanation we need to enclose it. We don't know who the agent of the action is. We don't even know why it was done. Instead of achieving closure, the story spreads over the landscape like a stain as we struggle to find a source of responsibility. In our time, responsibility without narratives has been consistently displaced by its enigmatic counterpart, conspiracy. Conspiracy works in tandem with narrative repression, the repression of who-has-done-what. We go back over the Kennedy assassination second by second, frame by frame, but there is a truth to it that we cannot get at because we can't be sure who really did it or what the motivations were. Everyone who claims to have closed the case simply establishes that the case will stay open. The result of dysfunctional narrative, as the poet Lawrence Joseph has suggested to me, is sorrow;

I would argue that it is sorrow mixed with depression or rage, the condition of the abject, but in any case we are talking about the psychic landscape of trauma and paralysis, the landscape of, for example, two outwardly different writers, Don DeLillo (in most of *Libra*) and Jane Smiley (in the last one hundred pages of *A Thousand Acres*).

Jane Smiley's novel has been compared to *King Lear*, and its plot invites the comparison, but its real ancestors in fiction are the novels of Émile Zola. *A Thousand Acres* is Zola on the plains. Like Zola, Jane Smiley assembles precisely and carefully a collection of facts, a naturalistic pileup of details about—in this case—farming and land use. As for characters, the reader encounters articulate women (including the narrator, Rose) and mostly frustrated inarticulate men driven by blank desires, like Larry, the Lear figure. Lear, however, is articulate. Larry is not. He is like one of Zola's male characters, driven by urges he does not understand or even acknowledge.

Somewhat in the manner of other naturalistic narratives, *A Thousand Acres* causes its characters to behave like mechanisms, under obscure orders. Wry but humorless, shorn of poetry or any lyric outburst, and brilliantly observant and relentless, the novel at first seems to be about 1980s greed and the destruction of resources that we now associate with Reaganism, a literally exploitative husbandry. Such a story would reveal clear if deplorable motives in its various characters. But no: The book is about the essential criminality of furtive male desire. With the revelation of Larry's sexual abuse of his daughters, in a recovered memory scene not so much out of Zola as *Geraldo*, it shifts direction toward an account of conspiracy and memory, sorrow and depression, in which several of the major characters are acting out rather than acting, and doing their best to find someone to blame.

The characters' emotions are thus preordained, and the narrator gathers around herself a cloak of unreliability as the novel goes on. It is a moody novel, but the mood itself often seems impenetrable, because the characters, including the men, are not acting upon events in present narrative time but are reacting obscurely to harms done to them in the psychic past from unthinkable impulses that will go forever unexplained. Enacting greed at least involves making some decisions, but in this novel, the urge to enact incest upon one's daughter is beyond thought, if not the judicial system, and, in turn, creates consequences that are beyond thought. Rose herself lives in the shadow of thought. Throughout much of the book she is unaccountable, even to herself, by virtue of having been molested by her father. This is dysfunctional narrative as literary art, a novel that is also very much an artifact of *this* American era.

Watergate itself would have remained narratively dysfunctional if the tapes hadn't turned up, and, with them, the "smoking gun"—notice, by the way, the metaphors that we employ to designate narrative responsibility, the naming and placing of the phallically inopportune protagonist at the center. The arms-for-hostages deal is still a muddled narrative because various political functionaries are taking the fall for what the commander in chief is supposed to have decided himself. However, the commander in chief was not told; or he forgot; or he was out of the loop; or he didn't understand what was said to him. The buck stops here? In recent history, the buck doesn't stop anywhere. The buck keeps moving, endlessly. Perhaps we are in the era of the endlessly recirculating buck, the buck seeking a place to stop, like a story that cannot find its own ending.

We have been living in a political culture of disavowals. Disavowals follow from crimes for which no one is capable of claiming responsibility. Mistakes and crimes tend to create narratives, however, and they have done so from the time of the Greek tragedies. How can the contemporary disavowal movement not affect those of us who tell stories? We begin to move away from fiction of protagonists and antagonists into another mode, another model. It is hard to describe this model but I think it might be called the fiction of finger-pointing, the fiction of the quest for blame. It often culminates with a scene in a court of law.

In such fiction, people and events are often accused of turning the protagonist into the kind of person the protagonist is, usually an unhappy person. That's the whole story. When blame has been assigned, the story is over. In writing workshops, this kind of story is often the rule rather than the exception. Probably this model of storytelling has arisen because sizable population groups in our time feel confused and powerless, as they often do in mass societies when the mechanisms of power are carefully masked. For people with irregular employment and mounting debts and faithless partners and abusive parents, the most interesting feature of life is its unhappiness, its dull constant weight. But in a commodity culture, people are *supposed* to be happy. It's the one myth of advertising. You start to feel cheated if you're not happy. In such a consumerist climate, the perplexed and unhappy don't know what their lives are telling them, and they don't feel as if they are in charge of their own existence. No action they have ever taken is half as interesting to them as the consistency of their unhappiness.

Natural disasters, by contrast—earthquakes and floods—are narratively satisfying. We know what caused the misery, and we usually know what we can do to repair the damage, no matter how long it takes.

But corporate and social power, any power carefully masked and made conspiratorial, puts its victims into a state of frenzy, a result of narrative dysfunction. Somebody must be responsible for my pain. Someone *will* be found. Someone, usually close to home, *will* be blamed. TV loves dysfunctional families. Dysfunctional S&Ls and banks and corporate structures are not loved quite so much. They're harder to figure out. They like it that way. In this sense we have moved away from the naturalism of Zola or Frank Norris or Dreiser. Like them, we believe that people are often helpless, but we don't blame the corporations anymore. We blame the family, and we do it on afternoon TV talk shows, like *Oprah.*

Afternoon talk shows have only apparent antagonists. Their sparring partners are not real antagonists because the bad guys usually confess and then immediately disavow. The trouble with narratives without antagonists or a counterpoint to the central character—stories in which no one ever seems to be deciding anything or acting upon any motive except the search for a source of discontent—is that they tend formally to mirror the protagonists' unhappiness and confusion. Stories about being put-upon almost literally do not know what to look at. The visual details are muddled or indifferently described or excessively specific in nonpertinent situations. In any particular scene, everything is significant, and nothing is. The story is trying to find a source of meaning, but in the story everyone is disclaiming responsibility. Things have just happened.

When I hear the adjective "dysfunctional" now, I cringe. But I have to use it here to describe a structural unit (like the banking system, or the family, or narrative) whose outward appearance is intact but whose structural integrity has been compromised or has collapsed. No one is answerable from within it. Every event, every calamity, is unanswered, from the S&L collapse to the Exxon Valdez oil spill.

So we have created for ourselves a paradise of lawyers: We

have an orgy of blame-finding on the one hand and disavowals of responsibility on the other.

All the recent debates and quarrels about taking responsibility as opposed to being a victim reflect bewilderment about whether in real life protagonists still exist or whether we are all minor characters, the objects of terrible forces. Of course, we are often both. But look at *Montel Williams,* or *Oprah.* (I have, I do, I can't help it.) For all the variety of the situations, the unwritten scripts are often similar. Someone is testifying because s/he's been hurt by someone else. The pain-inflicter is invariably present and accounted for onstage, and sometimes this person admits, abashedly, to inflicting the ruin: cheating, leaving, abusing, or murdering. Usually, however, there's no remorse or shame. Some other factor caused it: bad genes, alcoholism, drugs, or—the cause of last resort—Satan. For intellectuals it may be the patriarchy: some devil or other, but at least an *abstract* devil. In any case, the malefactor may be secretly pleased: s/he's on television and will be famous for fifteen minutes.

The audience's role is to comment on what the story means and to make a judgment about the players. Usually the audience members disagree and get into fights. The audience's judgment is required because the dramatis personae are incapable of judging themselves. They generally will not say that they did what they did because they wanted to, or because they had *decided* to do it. The story is shocking. You hear gasps. But the participants are as baffled and as bewildered as everyone else. So we have the spectacle of utterly perplexed villains deprived of their villainy. Villainy, properly understood, gives someone a largeness, a sense of scale. It seems to me that this sense of scale has probably abandoned us.

What we have instead is not exactly drama and not exactly therapy. It exists in that twilight world between the two, very

much of our time, where deniability reigns. Call it therapeutic
narration. No verdict ever comes in. Every verdict is appealed.
No one is in a position to judge. The spectacle makes the mind
itch as if from an ideological rash. Hour after hour, week after
week, these dysfunctional narratives are interrupted by commercials (on the Detroit affiliates) for lawyers.

But wait: Isn't there something deeply interesting and moving
and sometimes even beautiful when a character acknowledges
an error? And isn't this narrative mode becoming something of
a rarity?

Most young writers have this experience: They create characters who are imaginative projections of themselves, minus
the flaws. They put this character into a fictional world, wanting that character to be successful and—to use that word
from high school—*popular*. They don't want these imaginative projections of themselves to make any mistakes, wittingly
or, even better, unwittingly, or to demonstrate what Aristotle
thought was the core of stories, flaws of character that produce intelligent misjudgments for which someone must take
the responsibility.

   What's an unwitting action? It's what we do when we have to
act so quickly, or under so much pressure that we can't stop to
take thought. It's not the same as an urge, which may well have
a brooding and inscrutable quality. For some reason, such moments of unwitting action in life and in fiction feel enormously
charged with energy and meaning.

   It's difficult for fictional characters to acknowledge their
mistakes, because then they become definitive: They *are* that
person who did *that* thing. The only people who like to see
characters performing such actions are readers. They love to see

characters getting themselves into interesting trouble and defining themselves.

Lately, thinking about the nature of drama and our resistance to certain forms of it, I have been reading Aristotle's *Poetics* again and mulling over his definition of what makes a poet. A poet, Aristotle says, is first and foremost a maker, not of verses, but of plots. The poet creates an imitation, and what he imitates is an action.

It might be useful to make a distinction here between what I might call "me" protagonists and "I" protagonists. "Me" protagonists are largely objects—objects of impersonal forces or the actions of other people. They are central characters to whom things happen. They do not initiate action so much as receive it. They are largely reactionary, in the old sense of that term, and passive. They are figures of fate and destiny, and they tend to appear during periods of accelerated social change, such as the American 1880s and 1890s, and again in the 1980s.

The "I" protagonist, by contrast, makes certain decisions and takes some responsibility for them and for the actions that follow from them. This does not make the "I" protagonist admirable by any means. It's this kind of protagonist that Aristotle is talking about. Such a person, Aristotle says, is not outstanding for virtue or justice, and s/he arrives at ill fortune not because of any wickedness or vice, but because of some mistake that s/he makes. There's that word again, "mistake."

Sometimes—if we are writers—we have to talk to our characters. We have to try to persuade them to do what they've only imagined doing. We have to nudge but not force them toward situations where they will get into interesting trouble, where they will make interesting mistakes that they may take responsibility for. When we allow our characters to make mistakes, we release them from the grip of our own authorial narcissism. That's wonderful for them, it's wonderful for us, but it's best of all for the story.

A few instances: I once had a friend in graduate school who gave long, loud, and unpleasantly exciting parties in the middle of winter. He and his girlfriend usually considered these parties unsuccessful unless someone did something shocking or embarrassing or both—something you could talk about later. He lived on the third floor of an old house in Buffalo, New York, and his acquaintances regularly fell down the front and back stairs.

I thought of him recently when I was reading about Mary Butts, an English writer of short fiction who lived from 1890 to 1937. Her stories have now been reissued in a collection called *From Altar to Chimneypiece*. Virgil Thomson, who was gay, once proposed marriage to her, and says the following about her in his autobiography:

> I used to call her the "storm goddess," because she was at her best surrounded by cataclysm. She could stir up others with drink and drugs and magic incantations, and then when the cyclone was at its most intense, sit down at calm center and glow. All of her stories are of moments when the persons observed are caught up by something, inner or outer, so irresistible that their highest powers and all their lowest conditionings are exposed. The resulting action therefore is definitive, an ultimate clarification arrived at through ecstasy.

As it happens, I do not think that this is an accurate representation of Mary Butts's stories, which tend to be about crossing thresholds and stumbling into very strange spiritual dimensions. But I am interested in Thomson's thought concerning definitive action because I think the whole concept of definitive action is meeting up with considerable cultural resistance these days.

Thomson, describing his storm goddess, shows us a temptress, a joyful, worldly woman, quite possibly brilliant and bad to the bone. In real life people like this can be insufferable. Marriage to such a person would be a relentless adventure. They're constantly pushing their friends and acquaintances to lower their defenses and drop their masks and do something for which they will probably be sorry later. They like it when anyone blurts out a sudden admission, or acts on an impulse and messes up conventional arrangements. They like to see people squirm. They're *gleeful.* They prefer Bizet to Wagner; they're more Carmen than Sieglinde. They like it when people lunge at a desired object, and cacophony and wreckage are the result.

The morning after, you can say, "Mistakes were made," but with the people I've known, a phrase like "Mistakes were made" won't even buy you a cup of coffee. There is such a thing as the poetry of a mistake, and when you say, "Mistakes were made," you deprive an action of its poetry, and you sound like a weasel. When you say, "I fucked up," the action retains its meaning, its sordid origin, its obscenity, and its poetry. Poetry is quite compatible with obscenity.

Chekhov says in two of his letters, ". . . shun all descriptions of the characters' spiritual state. You must try to have that state emerge from their actions. . . . The artist must be only an impartial witness of his characters and what they said, not their judge." In Chekhov's view, a writer must try to release the story's characters from the aura of judgment that they've acquired simply because they're fictional.

In an atmosphere of constant moral judgment, characters are not often permitted to make interesting and intelligent mistakes and then to acknowledge them. The whole idea of the "intelligent mistake," the importance of the mistake made on an impulse, has gone out the window. Or, if fictional characters do make such mistakes, they're judged immediately and without appeal. One thinks of the attitudes of the aging Tolstoy and of his hatred of Shakespeare's and Chekhov's plays, and of his obsessive moralizing. He especially hated *King Lear*. He called it stupid, verbose, and incredible, and thought the craze for Shakespeare was like the tulip craze, a matter of mass hypnosis and "epidemic suggestion."

In the absence of any clear moral vision, we get moralizing instead. Moralizing in the 1990s has been inhibiting writers and making them nervous and irritable. Here is Mary Gaitskill, commenting on one of her own short stories, "The Girl on the Plane," in a recent *Best American Short Stories*. An account of a gang rape, the story apparently upset quite a few readers.

> In my opinion, most of us have not been taught how to be responsible for our thoughts and feelings. I see this strongly in the widespread tendency to read books and stories as if they exist to confirm how we are supposed to be, think, and feel. I'm not talking wacky political correctness. I'm talking mainstream. . . . Ladies and gentlemen, please. Stop asking "What am I supposed to feel?" Why would an adult look to me or to any other writer to tell him or her what to feel? You're not *supposed* to feel anything. You feel what you feel.

Behind the writer's loss of patience one can just manage to make out a literary culture begging for an authority figure, the same sort of figure that Chekhov refused for himself. Mary Gaitskill's interest in bad behavior and adulthood is that of the observer, not the judge. Unhappy readers want her to be both, as if stories should come prepackaged with discursive authorial opinions about her own characters. Her exasperation is a reflection of C. K. Williams's observation that in a period of dysfunctional narratives, the illogic of feeling erodes the logic of stories. When people can't make any narrative sense of their own feelings, readers start to ask writers to tell them what they are supposed to feel. They want moralizing polemics. Reading begins to be understood as a form of personal therapy or political action. In such an atmosphere, already moralized stories are more comforting than stories in which characters are making complex or unwitting mistakes. In such a setup, *Uncle Tom's Cabin* starts to look better than any other nineteenth-century American novel.

Marilynne Robinson, in her essay "Hearing Silence: Western Myth Reconsidered," calls the already moralized story, the therapeutic narrative, part of a "mean little myth" of our time. She notes, however, that "we have ceased to encode our myths in narrative as that word is traditionally understood. Now they shield themselves from our skepticism by taking on the appearance of scientific or political or economic discourse. . . ." And what is this "mean little myth"?

> One is born and in passage through childhood suffers some grave harm. Subsequent good fortune is meaningless because of this injury, while subsequent misfortune is highly significant as the consequence of this injury. The work of one's life is to discover and name the harm one has suffered.

This is, as it happens, a fairly accurate representation of the mythic armature of *A Thousand Acres*.

As long as this myth is operational, one cannot act, in stories or anywhere else, in a meaningful way. The injury takes for itself all the meaning. The injury *is* the meaning, although it is, itself, opaque. All achievements, and all mistakes, are finessed. There is no free will. There is only acting out, the acting out of one's destiny. But acting out is not the same as acting. Acting out is behavior that proceeds according to a predetermined, invisible pattern created by the injury. The injury becomes the unmoved mover, the replacement for the mind's capacity to judge and to decide. One thinks of Nixon here: the obscure wounds, the vindictiveness, the obsession with enemies, the acting out.

It has a feeling of Calvinism to it, of predetermination, this myth of injury and predestination. In its kingdom, sorrow and depression rule. Marilynne Robinson calls this mode of thought "bungled Freudianism." It's both that and something else: an effort to make pain acquire some comprehensibility so that those who feel helpless can at least be illuminated. But unlike Freudianism it asserts that the source of the pain can never be expunged. There is no working through of the injury. It has no tragic joy because, within it, all personal decisions have been made meaningless, deniable. It is a life fate, like a character disorder. Its politics cannot get much further than gender injury. It cannot take on the corporate state.

Confronted with this mode, I feel like an Old Leftist. I want to say: The Bosses are happy when *you* feel helpless. They're pleased when you think the source of your trouble is your family. They're delighted when you give up the idea that you should band together for political action. They'd rather have you feel helpless. They even like addicts, as long as they're mostly out of sight. After all, addiction is just the last stage of consumerism.

And I suppose I am nostalgic—as a writer, of course—for stories with mindful villainy, villainy with clear motives that any adult would understand, bad behavior with a sense of scale that would give back to us our imaginative grip on the despicable and the admirable and our capacity to have some opinions about the two. Most of us are interested in characters who willingly give up their innocence and start to act like adults, with complex and worldly motivations. I am fascinated when they do so, when they admit that they did what they did for good and sufficient reasons. At such moments the moral life becomes intelligible. It also becomes legibly political. If this is the liberal fallacy, this sense of choice, then so be it. (I know that people *do* get caught inside systems of harm and cannot maneuver themselves out—I have written about such situations myself—but that story is hardly the only one worth telling.)

It does seem curious that in contemporary America—a place of considerable good fortune and privilege—one of the most favored narrative modes from high to low has to do with disavowals, passivity, and the disarmed protagonist. Possibly we have never gotten over our American romance with innocence. We would rather be innocent than worldly and unshockable. Innocence is continually shocked and disarmed. But there is something wrong with this. No one can go through life perpetually shocked. It's disingenuous. Writing in his journals, Thornton Wilder notes, "I think that it can be assumed that no adults are ever really 'shocked'—that being shocked is always a pose." If Wilder's claim is even half true, then there is some failure of adulthood in contemporary American life. Our interest in victims and victimization has finally to do with our constant ambivalence about power, about being powerful, about wanting to be powerful but not having to acknowledge the buck stopping at our desk.

Romantic victims and disavowing perpetrators land us in a peculiar territory, a sort of neo-Puritanism without the backbone of theology and philosophy. After all, *The Scarlet Letter* is about disavowals, specifically Dimmesdale's, and the supposed "shock" of a minister of God being guilty of adultery. Dimmesdale's inability to admit publicly what he's done has something to do with the community—i.e., a culture of "shock"—and something to do with his own pusillanimous character.

The dialectics of innocence and worldliness have a different emotional coloration in British literature, or perhaps I am simply unable to get Elizabeth Bowen's *The Death of the Heart* out of my mind in this context. Portia, the perpetual innocent and stepchild, sixteen years old, in love with Eddie, twenty-three, has been writing a diary, and her guardian, Anna, has been reading it. Anna tells St. Quentin, her novelist friend, that she has been reading it. St. Quentin tells Portia what Anna has been doing. As it happens, Portia has been writing poisonously accurate observations about Anna and her husband, Thomas, in the diary. Anna is a bit pained to find herself so neatly skewered.

Bowen's portrait of Portia is beautifully managed, but it's her portrayal of Anna that fascinates me. Anna cannot be shocked. A great character you would never think of describing as "nice" or "likable," she is only what fictional characters should be—interesting. Everything she has done, she admits to. In the sixth chapter of the novel's final section, she really blossoms: Worldly, witty, rather mean, and absolutely clear about her own faults, she recognizes the situation and her own complicity in it. She may be sorry, but she doesn't promise to do better. Portia is the one who is innocent, who commands the superior virtues. Speaking of reading private diaries, Anna says, "It's the sort of thing I do do. Her diary's very good—you see, she has got us taped. . . . I don't say it has changed the course of my life, but it's given me a rather more disagreeable feeling about being alive—or, at least, about being me."

That "disagreeable feeling" seems to arise not only from the diary but from Anna's wish to read it, to violate it. Anna may feel disagreeable about being the person she is, but she does not say that she could be otherwise. She is honorable about her faults. She is the person who does what she admits to. As a result, there is a clarity, a functionality to Bowen's narrative that becomes apparent because everybody admits to everything in it and then gives their reasons for doing what they've done. Their actions have found a frame, a size, a scale. As bad as Anna may be, she is honest.

Anna defines herself, not in the American way of reciting inward virtues, but in a rather prideful litany of mistakes. In her view, we define ourselves at least as much by our mistakes as by our achievements. In fictional stories, mistakes are every bit as interesting as achievements are. They have an equal claim upon truth. Perhaps they have a greater one, because they are harder to show, harder to hear, harder to say. For that reason, they are rare, which causes their value to go up.

Speaking of a library book that is eighteen years overdue, but which she has just returned, the narrator of Grace Paley's story "Wants" says, "I didn't deny anything." She pays the thirty-two-dollar fine, and that's it. One of the pleasures of Paley's stories derives from their freedom from denial and subterfuge. Their characters explain themselves but don't bother to excuse themselves. City dwellers, they don't particularly like innocence, and they don't expect to be shocked. When there's blame, they take it. When they fall, they have reasons. They don't rise. They just get back on their feet, and when they think about reform, it's typically political rather than personal. For one of her characters, this is the "powerful last-half-of-the-century way." Well, it's nice to think so. Free of the therapeutic impulse, and of the recovery movement, and of Protestantism generally, her characters nevertheless *like* to imagine various social improvements in the lives of the members of their community.

Dysfunctional narratives tend to begin in solitude and they tend to resist their own forms of communication. They don't have communities so much as audiences of fellow victims. There is no polite way for their narratives to end. Richard Nixon, disgraced, resigned, still flashing the V-for-victory from the helicopter on the White House lawn, cognitively dissonant to the end, went off to his enforced retirement, where, tirelessly, year after year, in solitude, he wrote his accounts, every one of them meant to justify and to excuse. The title of his last book was apt: *Beyond Peace.*

On Defamiliarization

We start, this time, at a funeral. It's April. I'm sitting at the back of a church, where a memorial service is being staged for someone I did not know well. My responsibility is simple: to swell the crowd. I am present in the group of mourners for the benefit of the family, some of whose members I *do* know. For once, I am a willing statistic in a head count. Such a role makes almost anyone uneasy about social life: I mean the disturbing manner in which publicly displayed feelings tend to become stagy and to turn whatever surrounds them into theater. Contemporary poetry readings usually have this quality. Likewise the boy's-night-out and the business lunch and the bridal shower. They often have a kind of acted-out, scripted emotional life. In a similar way, family reunions sometimes shimmer with performance anxiety. In the midst of planned hilarity, we witness the show business of everyday life. Now, in this church, I have almost no feelings for, as the minister calls him, "the departed." Nevertheless, I am here.

With my attention wandering, I am trying not to look self-conscious. I pay attention to what people are wearing and am perversely pleased when I see food stains. I glance around at the

corners of this gloomy Gothic Revival church. The stained glass
is beautiful but in a stingy and pinched small-town Midwestern
manner. All the beauty in the Midwest, I think irritably, is on a
budget. A measured sampling of color in the stained glass was
all the past generations in this city would tolerate. But so far,
everything is going according to form: Episcopalians are in
charge. The cut flowers—lilies, I think—are out on display, the
organist has played Buxtehude and Bach, and the minister is
reading an elegy that is touching and probably, within its lim-
ited terms, accurate.

By the end of the service, I am glancing at the faces of the
mourners and doing my best to hide myself. I am beginning
to feel like an intruder, the orphan of good intentions, whose
feelings are at the opposite pole from sentimentality; this interesting and nagging condition has no name, at least in English:
You are supposed to feel some emotion, but can't. You are supposed to display feelings you don't actually have. This condition
is one of the many sources of collective social anxiety, and the
accumulation of performance strain in day-to-day life causes
an emotional disturbance that is visible on faces in the crowd: a
drawn, exhausted look from hours of compulsory insincerity.

People bred to social and urban organizations are forced to
confront the dribs and drabs of social make-believe almost by
the hour. Whitman recognized the problem and thought that
it was breeding and spreading in America after the Civil War
in the rise of oligopolistic business practices. Out of his delicate rage, in "Democratic Vistas," he described how men and
women lose themselves "in countless masses of adjustment." By
now it's a familiar story. Driving home, I think with guilty an-
noyance about the eulogy. My problem was that I hadn't known
the deceased well enough to know his failings—those features
by which I might have identified with him—and the litany of

praise only managed to distance him from me. I wanted a recital of his failures and oddities, which is exactly what Episcopalians do *not* hold up for display at funerals.

Most funerals contain a kind of narrative, a partial, inside narrative meant for the public or an idea of the public. The persona memorialized is remembered for his or her qualities, lovability, or achievements. But to misuse slightly a word from psychoanalysis, such a recitation is all overdetermined. All the arrows point in one direction: a characteristic feature of public rhetoric. In such a terminal narrative, everything fits. Because the details of the narrated life have a single function, the mourners feel that they have discharged a civic obligation. Tolstoy writes shrewdly about such survivor politesse in the opening section of "The Death of Ivan Ilych," but he cannot resist a barely controlled Tolstoyan irascibility at the truthlessness of such occasions, visible in the scurrying around, the unpleasantly mouselike qualities that he gives to Ivan Ilych's remaining family and friends, particularly Pavel Ivanovich.

If stories and novels used the selective form of funeral elegies, no one would read them. Characters who are entirely likable or admirable—who are remembered in the way that funeral elegies remember people—have a tendency to become either allegorical or bland. Narrated this way, they don't stay in the memory. Perversely, they vanish instead. By contrast, in fiction, characters are under no obligation to be good; they only have to be interesting. This statement is less tautological than it looks. As readers, we are asked to have feelings about people we haven't met and don't know, imaginary people who are strangers to us, and the only way to elicit those feelings involves using information about characters that doesn't fit a neat identity theme. Better yet, it may be unfavorable to them. The difference between fictional art and public rhetoric is that in fiction, the arrows point in *all* sorts of directions.

The problem I'm struggling to define arises with particular intensity when fiction is put to some social use. Social pressure makes demands and asks for model citizens, both in literature and outside of it. The obvious examples—the New Soviet Man in the era of socialist realism, the formulas of genre literature, including lonely beauties and mysterious romantic aristocrats—don't require much rethinking. But the problem for writers is that some social pressure of an obscure unanalyzable kind operates on characterization. Editors, agents, teachers, friends, and common readers are not slow to tell writers about what kind of characters they would like to see stalking through their pages. Even when these voices are absent, most writers feel their presence, like a star whose gravitational field bends the light that passes through it.

The first time I read Nathanael West's *Miss Lonelyhearts,* I was still in high school. I read the novel in one sitting in front of a window fan. Shrike's "first church of Christ, dentist" and his hysterical irony about art and redemption had a pleasing adolescent nastiness. I broke out into a sweat but not because of the heat. It was a readerly sweat. In a bit of a daze, I walked down the hill from our house to the lake and went swimming alone in the dark, which I had been instructed, countless times, never to do.

Miss Lonelyhearts himself made no sense to me as a character. That senselessness was pleasurable: He was like no one and nothing I'd ever encountered. At *his* funeral you would have no idea what to say, but in my mind a blank space full of misery and compassion waited for the likes of him. He instantly filled it. What a pleasure to recognize something without knowing *what* you're recognizing! He effortlessly took the shape of an emotion I knew but had no name for. In certain respects he was a character of pure contradiction. I couldn't have said that he was a thin shell built to house a relatively pure feeling, although that's a phrase that occurs to me now. What I loved about the book was that most of the rules, as far as I understood them, were being broken so that a memory stain resulted.

Miss Lonelyhearts has nothing to do with the pleasures of recognition. Its impatience with realism is quite feverish. The book has instead a peculiarly pure interest in the derangements of meaning. Recognition is forced to yield to a sort of comic-grotesque literary cartoon of the unnameable. Shock has something to do with this experience. So does the perception that profound emotions, at least in America, often *feel* cheap.

Unlike the austere purity of Beckett's unnameable, West's version of what lies beyond language is likely to come barging out of a comic book or a luncheonette. What he understands about the American sublime is that the aura, here, does not attach itself to churches or official monuments but to doggerel objects like mannequins, neon signs, and junk jewelry. In a letter, Rilke sneeringly refers to the products of America as "dummy life," but dummy life fascinates West because it's there that the spirit seems to have taken hidden refuge in America. West, of course, was obsessed by Hollywood, and with the semi-mechanical human beings in Los Angeles from whom the humanity seemed to have leaked.

A transition. Now it's February. A student of mine has turned in an eight-page story. The point of view is first person detached: In other words, an adult is telling (in the present tense, however) a story about what happened to her as a child. The story is written in six seemingly unconnected scenes, with space breaks but no transitions. A reasonably good workshop story, its milieu is a lower-middle-class family in a blue-collar suburb of Detroit.

In the first scene, a family is barbequing their Sunday afternoon meal in the backyard when the father interrupts the meal
to make a strange frantic speech about baseball. In the second
scene, he buys a clunker car, takes it to this same backyard, and
is about to fix it up when he decides to buy a speedboat, which,
after a few spins, he also transports to his backyard on a trailer.
He keeps buying objects that the family doesn't need. After a
while the yard is so crowded with junk that it's impossible to
barbeque there. In another scene, the father interrupts a picnic
by building too large a fire, using gasoline, and in yet another
he stops a Little League game by yelling gross obscenities at
the umpire, in front of the children. It gradually dawns on the
reader, in this case, me, that the story is about the father's alcoholism, a cause or effect of his bad behavior. In the subsequent
scenes, there's an all-American setting (a state fair, a bar-and-
grill) where the tone of placid companionable activity is ruined
by the father's misbehavior. It's like a Norman Rockwell painting with a charcoal-sketched demon raving away at the edges.

As I read through the subsequent scenes and began to think,
"Uh oh, he's going to be drunk again," the story's initial surprises began to seem less wonderful, even though its details were
excellent, and the story was never anything but truthful. But the
story had begun to read itself too early, and before very long it
was always and only about one thing, with the result that all the
details fit in perfectly. All the arrows pointed in the same direction. When all the details fit in perfectly, something is probably
wrong with the story. It is too meaningful too fast. Its meaning is overdetermined and the characters overparented. When
writers overparent their characters, they understand them too
quickly. Such characters aren't contradictory or misfitted. The
writer has decided what her story is about too early and has concentrated too fixedly on that one truth. Well, what's wrong with

the truth, and under what conditions does the truth grow un-dramatic, that is, without tension or instability? There's an issue here having to do with familiarity and writing, and anybody who has spent any time at all writing fiction has some intuitive sense of what this issue is.

This question is a remnant of the obsession of the Modernists with their own historical belatedness. The Modernists, many of them, experienced themselves as latecomers to virtually any scene that mattered. They felt that the truth had gotten stale, and they consequently came to dislike the word "truth." Erik Satie: "I was born very young in a very old time." This sense of things can be tracked already in the mid-nineteenth century with Flaubert, whose horror of clichés is simultaneously a spiritual nausea at arriving at all experience late, after everyone else has already gotten there, and a kind of revulsion at language that has been soiled by having been spoken first by the previous multitudes. Life, for Flaubert, is mostly a matter of making do with leftovers. Most experience, for him, has already started to rot, like a nearly inedible peach around whose decomposing sections you must eat with terrible, precise bites. I have always thought that this accounts for Flaubert's interest in affairs and in situations in which young men fall in love with married women. Charles Bovary, as a schoolboy, arrives late in class. Bouvard and Pecuchet arrive late at every subject on which they focus their easygoing haphazard attention.

One side-struggle of the wars of the avant-garde in the early decades of this century involved finding a way of introducing novelty into writing, the appearance of the newborn, the aesthetics of shock and surprise. Ezra Pound, that great demander, demanded, "Make it new." Diaghilev asked of Jean Cocteau, "Étonne-moi, Jean." The signs of success in this mode are the opening-night riot and the literary criminal. Norms are violated, the audience is shaken, and the artist-as-revolutionary gains tremendous authority. (In a certain light, this situation can seem to be all about artistic authority; after all, what composer today is looked up to as Stravinsky was?)

The anxiety of belatedness springs from an aesthetic restlessness, a troubled recognition that it is not always enough simply to tell a truth in art, especially if the truth has no dramatic tension or has lost its emotional force. The truth can get dull. It may fall into a nonnarratable condition. There is an odd, stranger-at-the-funeral sensation in the face of art that is truthful but too familiar, where the author is deeply moved, but no one else is. Most writers understand Chekhov's invitation to tell the truth *clearly* and *absolutely*; and writing that does not bother to tell the truth may fall into all sorts of errors of false dramatization, such as sensationalism or pornographic highlighting. In the late nineteenth century and the early part of this century artists became collectively worried—they noticed, all at once, that it was not enough to tell any story in a dramatic medium because its truth might have become familiar. In fact, all kinds of stories had become crushingly familiar.

What is the real relation between familiarity and contempt? This is by no means a simple question. Many marriage counselors think about this issue for long periods of time, as if it were a Zen koan. Familiarity, after all, is a kind of power, the power to predict and the power to abstract. It replaces the pleasure of the unknown with the pleasures of security. It signals that our our defenses are in place and are working. The kingdom is running smoothly. It's running smoothly because no one is learning anything. As in the story of the drunken father, all the details support the one central theme.

The assumption that some writers work from, that any valuable truth may essentially be dramatic, is clearly and unhappily mistaken. What I would argue is that the truth that writers are after may be dramatic only if has been forgotten first: if the story, in other words, pulls something contradictory and concealed out of its hiding place.

Anybody who has spent more than about twenty minutes in a fiction workshop will be familiar with this scene: Somebody's work is being critiqued. The piece is competent and about common life but rather conventional, without anarchy or excitement, and some devil's advocate in the room says, *Well, all right, the piece is competently written but, well it's sort of . . .* and there's a long pause while a substitute for the word "boring" is searched for. I've never heard participants in a writing workshop call a boring story "boring." It's bad form. They talk about dramatic construction or they say, "I had a problem with the pacing." All the same, it's obvious what they mean. And the writer of this piece, wounded all over again by life, eventually says, "But it really happened!" or "It's all true!"

A certain segment of the contemporary avant-garde has entered this particular fray by insisting on the principle of novelty or absolute innovation in technique or subject. If subjects about which you can say, "It's all true!" have become familiar, as all subjects must, then we shall concentrate on the language. Paraphrasing William Gass, there are no characters on the page, only words. Such a statement is unarguable but false to an experience of reading that concentrates on characters. It's like telling a bride on her wedding night that her spouse's body *really* consists of carbon molecules and hydrogen atoms and smaller subatomic particles such as quarks. It's true, but priggish, and beside the point. I admire visible language in fiction, but a fixation on it turns esoteric and mandarin quickly, and it does not really solve the problem of familiarity. It's like trying to fill an empty bank account by changing the pattern on the checks.

What's left of the avant-garde—there isn't much because anything can be packaged and made mainstream in this country—continues to insist on the (highly problematical) concepts of innovation and marginality. The old is relegated to the dustbin of history, and the new is briefly given its moment, usually by an outsider. This set of ideas replicates the production, use, and waste model of industrial consumption and capitalism. It also claims to be an attack on the bourgeoisie, but it uses a commodity model from free enterprise capitalism, and it packages itself with outrage. Outrage sells. Commercially successful commodified outrage is a dubious but by no means unknown category in American culture. One branch of the avant-garde has always thrived on throwing things out. To make it new, you have to haul the garbage away, and, in this particular ideology, there's a *lot* of garbage. Against this model of aesthetic clear-cutting one could propose a kind of ecology aesthetics, opposed to the obsession with innovation and waste. Conventionalized innovation, as Donald Barthelme, among others, knew very well, can become a tiresome cliché. "It is difficult," the narrator of Barthelme's "The Flight of Pigeons from the Palace" complains, "to keep the public interested . . . the supply of new ideas is not endless."

Right. The tradition of novelty, of ongoing necessary novelty has created a permanent confusion in this century in workshops and elsewhere. At the outer edge of experimentalism, innovation tends to put new lingerie on the banal. Many of us who are associated with writing programs have been made uneasy by these problems, and probably worry that we may be institutionalizing a series of conventional and conservative strategies for writing fiction. (That is what we are accused of, anyway, by the remnant of the avant-garde.) I myself have been made uneasy by these charges. But it seems to me that the concept of novelty, while not mistaken, is historically somewhat misleading, at least as a solution to the problem of familiarity, and I want to offer up another way to think about this matter by introducing, from Russian formalist criticism and the Russian critic Viktor Shklovsky, the concept of *defamiliarization,* which means to make the familiar strange, and the strange familiar. As another way of getting at this problem, I want to cite an idea from the notebooks of Gerard Manley Hopkins concerning the nature of the obsessive image, the "widowed" image, the image that sticks in the memory as if glued there.

Hopkins appeared to believe that images became memorable when some crucial part of their meaning had been stripped from them. Sometimes an obsessive image is the product of a trauma. The trauma cannot be remembered but has left its trace in misfit details. You may not remember your violent abusive uncle very well, but his blue glass ashtray or his decoy duck stays in your memory as if riveted there. The burden of the feeling is taken on by the objects. Shock is registered through these objects but the origin of the shock is protected. The objects, as a consequence, have a feeling of impatience and scale, as a fetish does.

Hopkins describes these obsessive images of objects as things for which he has not "found the law." They are unfulfilled in meaning, but they take up a lot of room in the memory as if in compensation. They seem both gratuitous and inexplicably necessary.

In 1917 Viktor Shklovsky published an essay called "Art As Technique," which, among its other tasks, is a commentary on Laurence Sterne's *Tristram Shandy.* Shklovsky concerns himself with numbness and boredom as problems of life and problems of art. He refers to the response of seeing the same thing several times as "algebrization." Algebrization is what we'd now call a coping mechanism. Algebrization is the process of turning an event or familiar object into an automatic symbol. It's like saying, *Oh, she's having another one of her crazy tantrums*, or, *Yeah, it's another goddamn freeway gridlock*. We protect ourselves from the force of her tantrum by turning it into an algebraic equivalent: Let x be the tantrum. Well, she's having another x. It's just one of those things she does. Here's Shklovsky:

> By this "algebraic" method of thought we apprehend objects only as shapes with imprecise extensions; we do not see them in their entirety but rather recognize them by their main characteristics. We see the object as though it were enveloped in a sack. We know what it is by its configuration, but we see only its silhouette. The object, perceived thus in the manner of prose perception, fades and does not leave even a first impression.

Shklovsky goes on to say that familiarity follows what he calls an economy of perception. You can't be equally attentive to everything. You have to budget your attention. That's how you survive. In order to drive to work, you can't treat every corner, every piece of perceptual material, as new, as if it were an image in a poem by Mallarmé. You have to drive the car; you have to get to work; you have to assume some familiarity with the problems you face or else you won't solve them, you'll just stare at them.

The process of defamiliarization is a technique for finding a certain kind of detail that resists the fitting of the object into a silhouette, that is, into a ready-made symbolization. Shklovsky advises a search for elements that don't fit—*misfit* details. He begins by arguing that if you have a familiar object or action to describe, you would do well not to name it, or to give it a new name, or to write as if you're seeing it for the first time, in a state of what might be called profitable forgetting. (Paul Valéry: "Seeing is forgetting the name of the thing one sees.") In one example, Shklovsky argues that Tolstoy, in his story "Shame," defamiliarizes a scene of flogging in this way: "to strip people who have broken the law, to hurl them on the floor, to rap on their bottoms with switches." Then Tolstoy remarks, "Just why precisely this stupid, savage means of causing pain and not any other—why not prick the shoulders or any part of the body with needles, squeeze the hands or the feet in a vise, or anything like that?" Tolstoy wants to be obtuse about torture—he doesn't get it. He doesn't see why anyone *should* get it.

In another example, Shklovsky shows how Tolstoy defamiliarizes a scene by shifting the perceptual center away from what you would expect, from a human being, in one particular case, to a horse in the story "Kholstomer." Shklovsky, in his discussion of this story, says, rather wonderfully, that "an image is not a permanent referent for those complexities of life which are revealed through it; its purpose is not to make us perceive meaning, but to create a special perception of the object—it creates a vision of the object instead of serving as a means of knowing it." A point of view that is off-center, a deflective point of view, may liberate the meanings of a story. As one gets older, the story of Hansel and Gretel becomes more interesting only when told from the point of view of the witch.

Shklovsky is talking about a process in which the object is stripped of its usual meanings. It is desymbolized, widowed. This removes the tyranny of meaning over event. Art that is overcontrolled by its meanings may start to go a bit dead: The images in the story will have a wilted quality, the feel of the vehement message about to leap over the experience. The image or scene will have been clapped onto a use function, and because everything has become pre-programmed, it becomes airless. Instead of being an experience, it has become a vehicle of opinions.

There is always something anarchic about the imagination: It likes to find details that don't belong, that don't fit. On the way to divorce court, we stop at the Dairy Queen. Your mean-spirited neighbor plays the violin and weeps while performing "Humoresque." Street gangs sometimes act like families, and families sometimes act like street gangs. The familiar gives way, not to the weird, but to the experience of a truth caught in mid-air. It produces the near laughter of recognition, as if every truth contains within it another truth that neatly contradicts it.

An example of this discovery of an opposite essence: Sherwood Anderson's story "Adventure," in *Winesburg, Ohio.* Anderson has a habit of pushing his situations toward desperation and then inserting a moment of bland stupidity in the middle of what would otherwise be melodramatic. Anderson was interested in lives in which desires and the satisfaction of those desires were relentlessly out of alignment. Emotional misalignment is one of his great subjects, what Montaigne called "soul error"—wanting what you know you can't have. Misalignment might be another subdivision of defamiliarization.

In the story "Adventure" there is a character named Alice Hindman. Early on in life she has an affair with a young man named Ned Currie. At the conclusion of their affair, he makes promises to her that he will return to town—he's leaving for Chicago—and marry her. Of course he has no intention of doing so. Not so extraordinary a story so far. So Alice waits back at home. During the day, she works in a dry goods store. She becomes obsessed with Ned. She prays to him. She thinks about him. Years pass. Ned does not return, but Alice continues to believe that he will.

One summer night, however, when she is twenty-seven years old, her belief system breaks down. She now knows that Ned won't come back and that she has been fundamentally—spiritually and sexually—humiliated. Outside, it's raining. The bottled-up force of her erotic feelings comes over her, and she gets an impulse to take off her clothes and to run naked in the rain in front of her house. And so she does. At this point, we are in what later became David Lynch Land, where the banal gives rise to melodrama and hysteria. (In Lynch's films, the grotesque, hallucinatory, and hysterical are the sole treasures of contemporary American life.)

But in Anderson's scene, as Alice is standing naked on the sidewalk, a man comes along, stumbling homeward. There are many ways of writing what follows, and they all depend on tone. The scene that Anderson wrote is both inevitable and un-expected and involves a genuine idea about loneliness. Alice, naked, rushes up to the man and says, "Don't go away! Whoever you are, you must wait!" And this man—who, the narrator tells us, is old and somewhat deaf—says, "What? What say?" And he goes on, tottering down the street. Defeated, Alice returns home, puts on her nightgown, and goes to bed, turning her face to the wall. She has had what amounts to a vision, and the vision is about the power of nakedness and sexuality in a culture of absentmindedness and obliviousness.

It is not the peculiarity or sensationalism of Alice's running in the rain that makes this a remarkable and memorable scene for me. What distinguishes it is that Anderson has pushed it out of sensationalism back into what I would call the resources of *surprising banality,* with that old deaf oblivious man, who is completely blind to the fact that he has encountered a naked

young woman on the sidewalk. A young naked woman is supposed to compel attention. In Anderson's society, and, for that
matter, in ours, there is the virtually universal and somewhat
Puritanical idea that a naked woman's body inevitably invites the
tyranny and the cruelty of the gaze. We hardly question it. But
Anderson is writing about blank lovelessness and sexual invisibility, and inside such a feeling is the perception that, when you
are desperate for attention, you will *not* get it. Attention is exactly
what Winesburg and the circumstances of Alice Hindman's life
deny her. As a woman and a human being, she has been erased
from Winesburg's map, and her body, her last semiotic appeal,
or vulnerability, or precious secret—it's all of these things, but it
will not be reduced to one meaning—carries the burden of her
longing, and becomes the record of her erasure.

There is a pileup of contradictory emotions in this scene:
sensuality and boredom and rage and revelation. The fallacy
of much fiction is that in any particular moment we are feeling one emotion, when in fact we are feeling many emotions
at once, many of them contradictory, such as lust and gloom.
But of course lust and gloom often go together *(Women in Love,
Ulysses, To the Lighthouse)*, as do depression and cheerfulness
(Evan Connell's brilliant *Mrs. Bridge*). What is a bored ecstasy
like? What does one feel in the midst of pessimistic hope? Is
there such a thing as a furious tenderness? Why are so many
psychopaths lovable? The monsters we have all known in our
lives are monsters almost by definition because they are often
not monsters, and we expect them to be one way, and they turn
out to be another. That's why we admitted them into our lives
in the first place.

Psychopaths, after all, are great charmers. Bad people are
good people who have gone on a sort of lifelong spiritual vacation, and who remember to be decent from time to time. In

Shklovsky's terms, we can defamiliarize our expectations by destabilizing our charcterizations, our narrative events, or our language, as say John Ashbery's poetry does. Ashbery's poetry is like an antique shop full of cast-off and secondhand phrases. The poetry itself is notable not for its new ideas—it doesn't have any—but for the new ways dull ideas and clichéd language can be employed. Ashbery himself combines a tone of full authority and total bewilderment.

Instead of making our narrative events and our characters more colorful, we might make them thicker, more undecidable, more contradictory and unrecognizable. In the example from Sherwood Anderson I've just used, the structure of the episode is close to a joke, but what is most lovable about Sherwood Anderson as a writer is that when pain is present in a story, Anderson never sees the joke. He will not—as Hemingway, for example, sometimes does—permit us the distance to regard their sufferings as comic.

Schopenhauer said that the business of the novelist is not to relate great events but to make small ones interesting. So much for *War and Peace*. All the same, it's not hard to see what he means. It's not the size of the event that counts in a story, it's the size of the frame built around that event. A wedding ring's size, in fiction as in a film, depends on how closely you're looking at it. The intensity of the attention changes the size of the frame and changes the sense of scale. Sometimes the intensity of this attention is a product of perceptual misalignment.

It may be more productive in telling a story to choose a narrator or a narrative point of view of someone who does not know what his own story means. Ford Madox Ford's *The Good Soldier* is the textbook example of the obtuse narrator, but there are many others. I'm not talking about unreliable narrators here so much as a narrator whose point of view doesn't mesh quite

properly with what s/he is seeing. Humbert Humbert, a culti-
vated but homicidally perverse European, has to find out about
American motel culture for the rest of us, as if he were a sort of
sexual Lewis and Clark. Benjy does not understand the South
and would not be able to read the book in which he appears,
The Sound and the Fury. Gatsby does not tell Gatsby's story;
Nick Carraway does. Nick does not know exactly what the story
means and allows it to go interestingly askew.

I do not read Russian, but I understand Shklovsky's term in
Russian, *ostraneniye,* literally to mean "making strange." The
key here may be to add an adverb: moderately strange, slightly
strange. The moderately strange in the middle of the ordinary is
the lens for focusing the ordinary. Without it, the ordinary has
nothing against which to define itself. The excessively strange
gets us into overcolorization, characters who are "characters,"
and actions with a Hollywood-like event inflation. What's needed,
in such cases, is what physicists call "renormalization."

You don't cry at the funeral unless you have had the time to know
the person who has died and to know that person in success as
well as failure. In some sense, taking on imaginatively the person who has died, you *become* that person. Defamiliarization
is finally more about the way in which we recognize ourselves
in an action and simultaneously see someone we don't recognize. Something has been widowed, images have been freed
from their meanings, something escapes us. We usually cannot recognize ourselves in a piece of fiction unless we have
been taken down a path in which we find ourselves split and
we meet ourselves coming in the other direction. Recognition
is re-cognitions: not finding ourselves where we expected to be
but where we did not expect to be found, and at a moment when
our defenses are down. We wake up next to someone we've lived

with for years but suddenly do not know. It's like that moment when, often early in the morning, perhaps in a strange house, you pass before a mirror you hadn't known would be there. You see a glimpse of someone reflected in that mirror, and a moment passes before you recognize that that person is yourself. Literature exists in moments like that.

Notes

Gerard Manley Hopkins, *Journals and Papers*. Edited by Humphrey House (London: Oxford University Press, 1959), pp. 193–194. I am following a discussion of the widowed image in Irving Massey, *Find You the Virtue: Ethics, Image and Desire in Literature* (Fairfax: The George Mason University Press, 1987): 153–155.

Viktor Shklovsky, "Art As Technique," in *Russian Formalist Criticism: Four Essays*. Translated and edited by Lee T. Lemon and Marion J. Reis (University of Nebraska Press, 1965).

Against Epiphanies

I've just had a major revelation.

These words typically fill me with dread. I have spent much of my life among the officially unconverted, but even they have their secret faiths and scrappy household gods. They, too, have visions. In social situations, piety is sometimes attached to some unusual articles of belief, and listening to descriptions of those beliefs can be a tricky business. The listener may never find the correct tone in which to respond, especially when agreement or disagreement are somehow beside the point.

When the large beliefs give way, the smaller ones are sometimes felt with an almost intolerable fervor. I once knew an ex-Catholic, a former altar boy, who was capable of lecturing me, and almost anyone else, at length about the benefits of cold-pressed salad oils. The emotion and rhetoric had a certain learned eloquence and were exalted but relentlessly applied to a pathetically diminished subject. The feeling for proportion was off. (Also a characteristic of television commercials, where love songs like "Nobody Does It Like You" are applied to Hoover vacuum cleaners.) In a relentlessly commercial culture, the

communication of our private meanings has been vaguely corrupted around the edges by the toxic idioms of merchandising.
Wanting to convey an inward sensation of the sacred, we find
ourselves skidding toward the usages of sales and marketing.
With the idiom already compromised, the experience of revelation begins to grow ever more unsteady: Its effect can be like
seasickness, but without the sea. In our age it tends to tremble
and vibrate, like any visitation. It breaks boundaries and jeop-
ardizes a feeling for scale.

A friend calls. She has been in emotional difficulty, but now,
she says, everything will be fine. She was awake last night, and
it came to her.

"What did?" I ask.

"Why I've been feeling this way," she says. "My troubles.
Suddenly I realized it."

So I asked what it was. She had been granted a revelation,
and now she was passing it on, like a virus, to me. I didn't believe that her explanations were the right ones, but I kept my
opinions quiet. I made nondirective noises, the sounds of telephone tact. Besides, who was I to comment? Who was I to say
that it wasn't the zinc in the vitamin pills, or the dust in the air,
or the selfish violence of men, or the unimpeachable banality of
the Midwest that had caused her anguish?

Suddenly I realized . . .

The language of literary epiphanies naturally has something
in common with the rhetoric of religious revelation. The veil of
appearances is pulled aside and an inner truth is revealed. A moment of radiant vision brings forth the sensation if not the content of meaning. An epiphany, in a traditional religious context,
was the showing forth of the divinity of the Christ child. It was,

quite literally, an awful moment. Awe governed it. To adapt this
solemn moment for literary purposes, as James Joyce wished to
do, was a Promethean gesture: It was an attempt to steal the fires
of religion and place them, still burning, in literature.

Consider this statement of the condition in Joyce's *Stephen
Hero*:

> By an epiphany he meant a sudden spiritual manifestation,
> whether in the vulgarity of speech or of gesture or in a memo-
> rable phase of the mind itself. . . . He told Cranly that the clock
> of the Ballast Office was capable of an epiphany. . . . —Imagine
> my glimpses at that clock as the gropings of a spiritual eye
> which seeks to adjust its vision to its exact focus. The mo-
> ment the focus is reached the object is epiphanized. It is just
> in this epiphany that I find the third, the supreme quality of
> beauty. . . . First we recognize that the object is *one* integral
> thing, then we recognize that it is an organized, composite
> structure, a *thing* in fact; finally, when the relation of the parts
> is exquisite, when the parts are adjusted to the special point,
> we recognize that it is *that* thing which it is. Its soul, its what-
> ness, leaps to us from the vestment of its appearance. The soul
> of the commonest object, the structure of which is so adjusted,
> seems to us radiant. The object achieves its epiphany.

The relation between this showing forth of the object's being
and the focus that the viewer brings to it is reciprocal. When
the act of attention is turned upon oneself, the self, through a
moment of seeing-in, an insight, may become radiant. But in
this formulation it can only be achieved through a sort of intellectual and spiritual discipline.

As a writer, Joyce never quite lost his vocation for the priest-
hood. The passage quoted above has retained its debt to Catholic
theology, particularly Aquinas, but has been iced over with the

slightly hectoring tone that Joyce gives to Stephen's pronounce-
ments. Like several of the Modernists, Joyce wished to convert
the drabness of truth-to-life detailing in narrative into a condition of inward revelation and resplendence. The passage from
Stephen Hero is a heroic statement of the manner in which a
drab city object can be converted into an essence, an object of
beauty.

Most of Joyce's writings involve a conversion of one kind or
another, both in substance and in style. The stories in *Dubliners*
are astonishingly detailed, but they continually aim for a climactic moment of brilliant transforming clarification. The clarification happens on the page, even if it does not become visibly
apparent to the characters. The stories aim for this effect because
the lives Joyce is putting on display might be insufferable to con-
template otherwise, or, rather, they would exist in a condition of
unimproved Naturalism. One such transformation arrives by
means of the moment of conclusive insight, the ripping away of
the veil of appearance, given to the narrator of "Araby" and to
Gabriel Conroy at the end of "The Dead."

Here is the ending of "Araby," in which the narrator arrives
at the little fair after it has closed, hoping to get a present for the
girl for whom he has an infatuation. He stands before a vendor:

> I lingered before her stall, though I knew my stay was useless,
> to make my interest in her wares seem the more real. Then I
> turned away slowly and walked down the middle of the ba-
> zaar. I allowed the two pennies to fall against the sixpence
> in my pocket. I heard a voice call from one end of the gal-
> lery that the light was out. The upper part of the hall was now
> completely dark.
>
> Gazing up into the darkness I saw myself as a creature
> driven and derived by vanity; and my eyes burned with an-
> guish and anger.

This miraculous and much-quoted passage manages to convey the bittersweet isolation of adolescence without quite yielding to it. It's as if the outer world gradually shuts itself off switch by switch, echo by echo, leaving the boy in his one burning isolated spotlight on his small diminished stage. He has become visible to himself. This seems to me a very canny understanding of the self-conscious awkwardness of adolescence. In this spotlight the boy sees that the world is arrayed against him. But not only the world: He is arrayed against himself. Granted his insight, he now possesses a sort of heroic watchful wretchedness.

As in a dramatic lyric, the *I* stands squarely at the center of this experience, of this world. The boy is the pale knight-at-arms on the cold hillside, the Byron who has failed at every pose he has attempted to strike. To get this mixture of anger, pathos, desire, and insight mixed in the right proportions is the miracle of Joyce's short stories. The insight follows the images but is not secondary: It balances them. The insight feels transfiguring in the way that melancholy can be for those who are starting to understand the depths and the identifying marks of their own inwardness. It also feels newly discovered, despite its debts to Romantic poetry and the culture of Irish Catholicism.

Reading a passage like this one is a bit like reading Freud's *The Interpretation of Dreams*. It is the trickle that precedes the flood. When the middle classes discovered insight—revelation free of the obligations of organized religion—they made a serious investment in it, and the proportions so carefully watched over in *Dubliners* began, imperceptibly at first, I think, to be violated. The logic of unveiling has become a dominant mode in Anglo-American writing, certainly in fiction, particularly short stories. We watch as a hidden presence, some secret logic, rises to visibility and serves as the climactic revelation. (It may be visible to us but not to the characters; however most of the time, in contemporary writing, the characters not only see it, they announce it.) The world of appearances falls away, and essences show themselves.

The loss of innocence, and the arrival of knowingness, can become an addiction. Cultures with a fascination with innocence often cannot get enough of these moments.

Here, as another example, is the ending, the last paragraph, of John Cheever's "Goodbye, My Brother." The narrator is deploring the gloom and pessimism of his brother.

> Oh, what can you do with a man like that? What can you do? How can you dissuade his eye in a crowd from seeking out the cheek with acne, the infirm hand; how can you teach him to respond to the inestimable greatness of the race, the harsh surface beauty of life; how can you put his finger for him on the obdurate truths before which fear and horror are powerless? The sea that morning was iridescent and dark. My wife and my sister were swimming—Diana and Helen—and I saw their uncovered heads, black and gold in the dark water. I saw them come out and I saw that they were naked, unshy, beautiful, and full of grace, and I watched the naked women walk out of the sea.

This passage has its own narrative grace and fluidity, and an eloquence about essences in both the discursive insight at the beginning of the paragraph and the dramatic epiphanic image that ends it. It feels a bit like an aria, but the voice is under very little strain in singing it. Nevertheless, the materials are being pushed toward timelessness and myth (Diana and Helen) and grand gestures, even affirmations of faith, such as "the inestimable greatness of the race." The tessitura, the line of the melody, is much higher than it is in "Araby." I am conscious here, as I am not in "Araby," of the difficulty of putting this over. Women might not care for what is being done to and for women here. The passage is determined to be gorgeous without being lush. I think it succeeds, but just barely.

Some of the most beautiful stories ever written, at least in the last 150 years, follow this pattern. Several of the greatest ones in the literature of this century have endings that resemble those in "Araby" or "Goodbye, My Brother." But a mode that began with moves of elegant feeling and energy, particularly in stories that have to deal with worlds within worlds of urban or small-town or even familial hypocrisy can get stale. Worse than stale: rotten. The mass production of insight, in fiction or elsewhere, is a dubious phenomenon. However, in contemporary society almost anything can be mass produced and marketed, even insight. Especially insight. Because it is a private experience, it can't be debated or contested. Suddenly, it seems, everyone is having insights. Everyone is proclaiming them and selling them. Possibly we have entered the Age of Insight. Everywhere there is a glut of epiphanies. Radiance rules. But some of the insights have seemed disturbingly untrustworthy. There is a smell about them of recently molded plastic. At the level of discursive rhetoric, it is a bit like the current craze for angels. Perhaps, one is free to wonder, perhaps these are not true insights at all. What then?

This country has always harbored, and perhaps has always been fascinated by a certain variety of the isolated thinker—sometimes a genius, sometimes a crackpot, and sometimes a weird mixture of the two. The isolated thinker comes up with philosophies that depend, not on commonly agreed-upon observations, but on cranky insights. Thoreau is perhaps the best example, but Henry James, Sr., with his interest in Swedenborg and the occult, is another. We would probably not remember much about the writing of the elder Henry James if it weren't for the ways that his distrust of appearances became apparent in the fiction of his son.

Insights, in art and outside of it, depend on an assumption that the surface is false. That what one sees—the evidence of one's eyes—is at best a partial truth. That almost everyone has been mistaken. All cults, and the occult arts, assume this to be the case. The loss of innocence is partly a recognition that there are depths to things, that what you see is not always what you get. The pathos of this discovery is well known, especially among Americans and adolescents. But the fascination with false surfaces leads, fairly quickly, to a fascination with conspiracies. It is one thing to say that the surface is illusory. It's another to say that the illusion has been designed that way by fools or malefactors.

Conspiracy theorists thrive on epiphanies, insights, and revelations. The business of uncovering a conspiracy is very close to the mechanisms of literary production: It's why the word "plot" suits both of them. Something Else—the hideous prime mover, masterfully disguised—is in charge. When a conspiracy is unmasked, the insights that follow are peculiarly unsettling however, because all the truths that emerge are ugly. This is at variance with our hope that the truth, when it rises to the surface in a story, will be as beautiful as Cheever's swimmers walking out of the sea.

> *What good are insights? They only make things worse.*
> —Raymond Carver

Insights leave one stunned. Sometimes the vision causes the world to fall away, and sometimes the objects in that world take on a Promethean fire and radiance, but quite often the truth of things is so overpowering that one simply has nothing to do and nowhere to move. Following the radiance comes the immobility. Radiance doesn't need anyone to add anything to it. And sometimes the epiphanic insight is not so radiant. You discover that you are going to spend your life in Laundromats, fighting other people to get access to the dryers. In most stories, this moment, which is understood in our literary tradition to be important and climactic, carries with it a stop-time effect. When things just stop, the fire of insight inhabits the screen.

Insight is one of the last stands of belief in a secular age. I feel that I am saying something here that is both obvious and obtuse. Insight's connection to the loss of innocence, to a vestigially religious worldview, and to conspiracy theories, makes it particularly suited to a culture like ours that thrives on psychotherapeutic models, paranoia, and self-improvement. A belief that one is a victim will lead inevitably to an obsession with insight. There is really nothing wrong with any of this except for the conventions it is capable of fostering. The mass-marketing of literary epiphanies and climactic insights produces in editors and readers an expectation that stories must end with an insight. The insight-ending, as a result, has become something of a weird norm in contemporary writing.

The reason I find these developments baffling is that discursive insights are so rare, in my experience, that they seem freakish. Another reason I am baffled is that, in retrospect, I can say with some certainty that most of my own large-scale insights have turned out to be completely false. They have arrived with a powerful, soul-altering force; and they have all been dead wrong.

But, to paraphrase Cheever, if you take away fiction's insights, what do you have left?

Imagine, for the sake of the argument, two ways of approaching a story.

Suppose, in honor of the least visible of the Marx Brothers, we have before us a well-meaning apprentice writer named Zeppo. Let's suppose that Zeppo is writing a story with a conventional plot structure, one in which, following suggestions that go back for over two thousand years, he creates an introduction of oppositions, a deepening of those oppositions, a crisis, and a resolution. Zeppo has arranged his plot so that his protagonist, a charming gangster, has won the heart of the mayor's daughter. He is opposed in this love match by the mayor himself, who has allied himself with a rival group of gangsters. Near the end of the story there is a battle of some kind, and someone wins. From *The Decameron* to *Romeo and Juliet* to *The Godfather* and *Prizzi's Honor,* this story has held the attention of readers. The characters need not be distinguished by their intelligence or sensitivity. The poetry may be supplied by the narrator or by the eloquence of the participants. Eloquence isn't the same as sensitivity. The action itself may be intricate and beautiful in its understanding of character and milieu, but it need not be redemptive in any sense. What these characters do have is powerful desires. Also, there may be many coincidences that lead to violence.

But Zeppo has read Henry James's prefaces and Chekhov's letters and several volumes of Virginia Woolf's diaries and the last ten volumes of *Best American Short Stories.* He knows that his story is not especially subtle, although it is a page-turner, so he tears it up and starts over. In the story that Zeppo then writes, the charming gangster is transformed into a young man, who discovers during the time he is taking out a young woman, that his own father, whom he once idolized, has distant ties to certain elements of organized crime. This revelation leads the young man to a second revelation, namely, that there is a connection between adulthood and guilt, and that crime is sometimes a matter of moral ambiguity. Should he tell his wife-to-be?

Whether the gangster's son marries the young woman in this story may be less important than the boy's moment of recognition of who he is in relation to the guilt or innocence of the adult world.

In this story, the boy's youth is an important thematic ingredient, and it is also helpful if the young person is intelligent enough to experience a kind of revelation. What is sometimes (and condescendingly) called "sensitivity" has entered the picture. *The Godfather* also tells this story, the representative figure in this case being not a man but Kay Corleone, née Adams, Michael's girlfriend and subsequently his wife. And we find versions of this state of affairs in the insights granted to Nick Carraway in *Gatsby* or Catherine Sloper in *Washington Square* or Miranda in Katherine Anne Porter's "Old Mortality" or virtually all of the protagonists in J. D. Salinger's fiction or . . . many other characters in many other stories and novels. In this story the actions are less important than what is made of them in the protagonist's consciousness. The significance of the story has moved part or all of the way out of action into sensibility, and the product of action, in this model, is a kind of wisdom, often about hypocrisy. We have entered the thickets of the coming-of-age tale.

Writing the first story, Zeppo moves toward a dramatic climax in which the charming gangster engages in some appropriate conclusive action, usually violent. Having discarded that story, Zeppo moves toward a climactic moment in which the protagonist, who is now telling the story, says, in a moment of stunned clarity, "Suddenly I realized . . ."

In moving from story number one to story number two, Zeppo has relived the conversion that Henry James and James Joyce pioneered in the form of the Anglo-American short story when they steered it away from the plot structures tending to require a set of coincidences or connivances of circumstance, which they found unacceptably coarse. Versions of the coincidence story— with a suppressed narrative or a "poetic justice" ending—can be found in the work of O. Henry, Somerset Maugham, Rudyard Kipling, Stanley Elkin, and Roald Dahl. But insistence on action has caused this sort of story to reside most often in the movies, where sensitive protagonists and their insights are not as effectively dramatized as hot-blooded characters who take immediate steps to get what they want.

I have a feeling that the literary short story took up secular epiphanies because the movies didn't need them, or at least didn't require them as much as other more visible and dynamic narrative ingredients. Insight is a difficult quality to capture on film, and radiance, with its tendency toward visual bombast, is worse. But that's not the only reason. There's something here having to do with class. A professional-managerial class believes that it needs insights in order to survive. For the middle class, information and mental events are far more important than physical actions. Insights can lead to a sense of how things work and how they may be controlled, what a friend of mine used to call the "Bingo moment."

But I must confess a prejudice here, which is probably already apparent. I don't believe that a character's experiences in a story have to be validated by a conclusive insight or a brilliant visionary stop-time moment. Stories can arrive somewhere interesting without claiming any wisdom or clarification, without, really, claiming much of anything beyond their wish to follow a train of interesting events to a conclusion. I am begging the question by using the word "interesting" here, but not much. Nor do I think that the insight—if it does come—needs to be valid or true. Stories built from false insights have their own peculiar interest, particularly in a hard-sell society, all of whose economic pressures warp in the direction of secret knowledge that can be cannily merchandised.

One other trouble with epiphanic endings is that they have become a tic, a habit, among writers (and editors) of literary fiction. Insights provide a certain kind of closure, and, not to put too vulgar a point on it, a payoff. Radiance, after a while, gets routine. That old insight train just comes chugging into the station, time after time. Flannery O'Connor once said that her aunt felt that a story had not really ended unless, at the conclusion, someone was either married or shot dead. If you gave Flannery O'Connor's aunt a college degree, she might very well demand, instead, an epiphany at the end of a story. In most anthologies of short stories published since the 1940s, insight endings or epiphanic endings account for approximately 50 to 85 percent of all the climactic moments. I once received a letter from an editor of a respected literary journal who complained that the story I had submitted to him was unsatisfying because "the amount of insight given to the protagonist is not great enough to justify the quantity of narrative detail."

This is not a stupid critical objection. It has some traces of reader weariness. This reader has probably read too much fiction that hasn't led anywhere. The fatigue has been inscribed in the critical position. Notice that in this statement, narrative detail is assumed to require a justification. That's the postmodern impatient middle-class Puritan speaking, sick to death of one story after another.

You almost have to get outside of a culture tainted by Puritanism to talk about other kinds of endings. Almost.

Obvious point: Short stories end before novels do and therefore have a more critical relation to the immediacy of closure and what might constitute it. Arguable point: Characters in short stories, unlike the characters in novels, do not, as a rule, make long-term plans. They tend, instead, to be creatures of impulse.

The ending of the short story often does glance uneasily toward the future, but stories frequently try to keep both the past and the future bracketed and separate. The story form has an extraordinary capacity to sense what's been at stake in any action or encounter because it has a heightened feeling for immediate consequences. I want to lean here on the word "consequences." We can have stories of real consequence in which no discursive insight appears, or in which the insights are shown to be false (this is a kind of story one often finds in Borges). What if, as Raymond Carver argued, insights don't help and only make things worse? We can still see people acting meaningfully or stewing in their own juices or acting out of the depths of their bewilderment, and we can make of that what we will. A story, as Borges has shown, can be a series of clues but not a solution, an enfolding of a mystery instead of a revelation. It can contain the images without the attached discursive morality.

Bewilderment—in the moment before the insight arrives, *if* it arrives—has at least two very attractive features. One is its relation to comedy. The other is its solitary stubbornness.

Anti-epiphanic writing is perfectly capable of sneaking its own visionary eloquence through the back door, but it is usually at some pains to avoid the proclamation effect and the conclusiveness of vision or insight that I have been describing. It has been and probably will always be a kind of minority writing: quarrelsome, hilarious, and mulish. It is resistant to authority. Instead of a conclusive arrival somewhere, we end, or rest, at a garden of forking paths, or an apartment complex where no one knows how to start the car, but everyone has an opinion, possibly worthless, about the matter.

To line up with the anti-epiphanic is to withdraw from officialdom. Officials, and official culture, are full of epiphanies and insights and dogmas. One is free to be sick of that mode of discourse.

In James Alan McPherson's "Elbow Room," the concluding story in his book of that title, the narrative, the paraphrasable part of it, has to do with the courtship, marriage, and parenthood of Paul Frost, a young white man from Kansas, and Virginia Valentine, a young black woman from outside Knoxville. The story, however, has another level: the narrator's meditation on them and their baby and on his story generally, and his bemusement over his (possible) inadequacy in telling about the story "clearly." In the course of the story, Paul seems to metamorphose in some manner into a different kind of man (he is called a "nigger" twice), and the narrator makes a considerable point of not knowing exactly what his own story means, and in particular what has happened to his central characters.

But the story has a third voice as well: a representative of officialdom, an editor, whose comments, *in italics,* litter the story with demands for clarity and insight. Quite properly, this editor is faceless. We know nothing about him or her except for the nagging comments that s/he makes all the way through the story. This editor is a police-state formalist and keeper of the orders, and as such s/he has the first and last words, both of them indictments:

> *Narrator is unmanageable. . . . Insists on unevenness as a virtue. Flaunts an almost barbaric disregard for the moral mysteries, or integrities, of traditional narrative modes. This flaw in his discipline is well demonstrated here. In order to save this*

narration, editor felt compelled to clarify slightly, not to censor
but to impose at least the illusion of order.

Those "moral mysteries" sound like Stephen Dedalus talking. At the end of the story, the narrator disowns insight, after having been badgered by the editor-in-italics. "It was from the beginning not my story. I lack the insight to narrate its complexities. But it may still be told." Several sentences later, of course, the editor butts in again, with a final nagging insert: *"Comment is unclear. Explain. Explain."* Nevertheless, all the way through this tale, the editor has been obtuse about the complexities of racism, narration, identity, and storytelling, and has wanted these matters wrapped up and commodified, as if for an anthology to be used for pedagogical purposes. "Elbow Room" resists the editor's packaging, absolutely. It will not grant the editor— which after all may be an inner editor—the neatness of clarity, because any clarity concerning its events would be false to the shadings and nuances of Paul and Virginia's story and the narrator's own itchy involvement with it. It is the most complex American story I know about a resistance to the packaging of neat explanations of racism for the edification of readers. To the degree that the story resists that packaging, it gives back to its events the dignity of their own complexity.

The story is not, however, widely known as a classic. It shrugs off portentous declamations and in general resists the earth-shaking masterpiece tone, meant to impress and terrify. It sets before us, instead, the fictionality of all insight. What a relief.

Here is the totality of a story by Lydia Davis called "Disagreement," printed in *Indiana Review*:

> He said she was disagreeing with him. She said No, that was
> not true, he was disagreeing with her. This was about the screen

door. That it should not be left open was her idea, because of
the flies; his was that it could be left open first thing in the
morning, when there were no flies on the deck. Anyway, he
said, most of the flies came from other parts of the building:
in fact, he was probably letting more of them out than in.

This particular story is not from her book *Break It Down,*
although it would fit well in that collection of virtuoso oddball
exercises in comic and anguished skepticism. In that collection,
Lydia Davis seems, sometimes, to be reinventing the short-story
form each time that she sits down to write. (Most of the stories,
I should add, are longer than this one, but they are not so much
developmental as permutational; they do not advance on a line
so much as spin on a point, and report on what is glimpsed from
that particular angle before turning to a different angle on the
same point. They are not revolutionary so much as rotational.)
What she often produces is a report on a world in which insights are flattened by the exasperated monochromatic voice
into minimal observations that are then contested by other observations, reported in exactly the same manner.

These stories stare, critically, at their own language. They
are particularly interested in debased and public languages that
people are gleefully using without knowing what they mean.
Consequences arrive whose truth cannot be paraphrased because that particular language won't permit it.

There is probably a limit to how many of these stories can
be absorbed on their own terms before some readerly failure-to-
respond kicks in, but they have the virtue of their own obses-
siveness, and, often (as in "Disagreement") they process heated
exchanges through almost comically elaborate and distanced
syntax. "That it should not be left open was her idea, because
of the flies. . . ." The language of contract law, of hair-splitting,
of intelligence generally at its wit's end informs this and many

of her other sentences. These stories glimpse an opportunity in mangled Cartesian rationalism never to arrive at a still point of the turning world. The still point is screwed, almost literally, to the wall, and is forced to spin.

> If I were not me and overheard me from below, as a neighbor, talking to him, I would say to myself how glad I was not to be her, not to be sounding the way she is sounding, with a voice like her voice and an opinion like her opinion. But I cannot hear myself from below, as a neighbor, and cannot know how I ought not to sound, I cannot be glad I am not her, as I would be if I could hear her. . . .

That is from "From Below, as a Neighbor."

In these stories there is a gradual freezing of the narrative frame. It seems to me to involve a stop-time effect but without the accompanying discursive enlightenment, and it depends (in the examples I've given from McPherson and Davis) not on the resources of conflict resolution, but on the resources of quarreling. The quarrel is not resolved; the quarrel goes on; the quarrel becomes the life. But gradually the frame and the elemental ingredients of the story begin to freeze in their position. Raymond Carver's stories often seem to freeze at the end, particularly those unforgiving stories in *What We Talk About When We Talk About Love*. It is sometimes hard to tell if this effect is meant to be funny or not. The tone is so undecidable that one is free to laugh or fall into some other condition. There is a certain refusal to please the crowd that hardens into an attitude, a pose, and the hardening of an attitude can be comic, but only if you have a certain distance from it.

At the end of "Viewfinder," a man without hands, who goes door to door making a living by taking pictures of peoples' houses, makes the acquaintance of the narrator. The narrator, in his fashion, has been sitting and looking out of the window after his wife and children have left him. He has been brewing coffee and making Jell-O. He lets the man without hands use the bathroom and drink the coffee. It's "Cathedral" without the cathedral and the healing and the late-night lifting of the spirit, which is to say that it's quite a different story. At the end the narrator climbs onto the roof of his house, the sort of locale, given the altitude, where epiphanies often come from, at least in the suburbs. But instead of getting a view of things, the long view, for example, this is what the narrator gets, and what he does with it:

> It was then that I saw them, the rocks. It was like a little rock nest on the screen over the chimney hole. You know kids. You know how they lob them up, thinking to sink one down your chimney.
>
> "Ready?" I called, and I got a rock, and I waited until he had me in his viewfinder.
>
> "Okay!" he called.
>
> I laid back my arm and I hollered, "Now!" I threw that son of a bitch as far as I could throw it.
>
> "I don't know," I heard him shout. "I don't do action shots."
>
> "Again!" I screamed, and took up another rock.

Instead of having an insight, the narrator acts out. The story ends in the middle of an action, as the narrator picks up another rock. Anger can be its own poetry and does not need to be assuaged. One could say that the story has an exacting focus on its objects without extracting any radiance from them. This kind of story begins an action but does not complete it.

We find this in many other short stories. Perhaps my favorite practitioner of the mode is Dino Buzzati, in his collection *Restless Nights,* and in such stories as "The Falling Girl." The falling girl, at the beginning of her story, "leaned out over the railing and let herself go. She felt as if she were hovering in the air, but she was falling."

But she is not, as it happens, falling swiftly. She falls in fictional time, rather than real time. Events slow down for her and seem, gradually, to freeze. The effect is lyric and comic and rather tender. (It is not so tender with another practitioner of this mode, Italo Calvino, whose fiction enjoys trapping its protagonists in formal boxlike structures with violence-prone antagonists just outside.) Marta, the falling girl, has conversations with cocktail-party guests out on their balconies; she refuses the occasional flirtatious gesture; she continues to fall.

> A young man, tall, dark, very distinguished, extended an arm to snatch her. She liked him. And yet Marta quickly defended herself: "How dare you, sir?" and she had time to give him a little tap on the nose.
> The beautiful people, then, were interested in her and that filled her with satisfaction. She felt fascinating, stylish.

It does not take a particularly attentive reader to realize that Marta will never reach the ground, at least in this story. The action has started but has not, will not, complete itself, and the fall begins to convert itself into a sweetly suspended metaphor. Metaphor is holding Marta up in the air. No one is going to arrive anywhere in this story. We don't even end with Marta, but with an unidentified man musing about the falling women (he lives near the ground, and the girls have grown old by the time they fall past his floor). Their apartment is cheap, his wife says, because the girls have aged by the time they get there. The man sips his coffee. He thinks about his wife's observation. Perhaps it is not true. The story seems to end . . .

The epiphany was never meant to be used for merchandising and therapy. It is not easily adapted to a mass market. But practical measures have been applied. The job has been done. These

singular occasions of perception have become so ubiquitous that
a refusal of them seems not so much perverse as quietly heroic.
No one wants to be numbered among the lost, exactly, or among
those without the resources of insight; everyone wants to be saved.
It all has to do with the conditions of salvation. Sometimes it
may be better to muddle through, slow down the action, and put
on a few ironies for the time being. German literature right now
is exemplary in its employment of fastidious and lyrical irony.
It has to be. It's a correction. Just because there is no religion
around doesn't mean that the rest of us aren't under intense pressure to be saved these days, not when there is so much money to
be made in the saving of us. Now that the production of epiphanies has become a business, the unenlightened are treated with
sad pity, and with the little grace notes of contempt.

There are the happy ones on the ship, embarking, outward
bound. And then there are the rest of us, standing on the dock.

Sometimes readers are not going to be helped along by the
stories they read. Literature is not an instruction manual. For
obvious reasons, this is rarely noted in fiction. Denis Johnson's
narrator in "Car Crash While Hitchhiking," however, leaves
himself narratively in that story in detox at Seattle General
Hospital. He is hallucinating, flopping like a fish, and then on
his stomach, as the nurse injects him with what she says are
vitamins. Here is the last paragraph of the story:

> It was raining. Gigantic ferns leaned over us. The forest drifted
> down a hill. I could hear a creek rushing down among rocks.
> And you, you ridiculous people, you expect me to help you.

Talking Forks: Fiction and the Inner Life of Objects

for Irving Massey

About a third of the way through Ivan Turgenev's second novel, *Home of the Gentry* (1859), the hero, a luckless man named Lavretsky who has been suffering through a painful marriage and who will soon fall in love with a woman as unsuited to him as his wife has been, pauses for a moment to observe the flow of natural events outside in an open field. Lavretsky has not been a particularly gifted observer at any time in his life, at least until now. His obtuseness probably accounts for his tendency to love people who cannot love him back.

Because this is a Russian novel of the mid-nineteenth century, Lavretsky's gift of sight occurs on an estate. He is feeling bored and lazy. For the first time, it seems, he is paying some attention to things he cannot touch or eat. (The narrative has somewhat slyly let us know that he is overweight.) Calmly indolent in the middle of his unharvested crops, he begins to listen to gnats and bees. Half lost in all this vegetation, he sees brightly burnished rye and the oats that have formed (in Richard Freeborn's

translation for the Penguin edition) "their little trumpet ears."
Out of habit, he returns his conscious attention to himself and
thinks immediately of his miserable romantic attachments, but
then, as if his perspective has been subtly adjusted, he looks
again at the objects in front of him.

All at once the sounds die, and Lavretsky is "engulfed" in
silence. He looks up and sees "the tranquil blue of the sky, and
the clouds floating silently upon it; it seemed as if they knew
why and where they were going."

Russian literature has more than a few moments like this
when wisdom arises out of indolence. This particular one is
unusually eerie. Lavretsky has lost his industry, or maybe his
industriousness, and in this pre-industrious state he can see
self-contradicting objects that are metaphorically both ears and
trumpets, producers and receivers of sound that are playing only
in his imagination. In his laziness, Lavretsky hands over his feeling and thinking to the objects that constitute his environment,
and in this air-pocket of silence the clouds acquire consciousness
and a sort of intelligence. The passing of the clouds feels slightly
god-haunted, although no god is visible anywhere in the scene.

It seems important to me to resist reading this episode
through what we may know about large conceptual categories
or figures of the time, or later: Wordsworth, English Romantic
poetry, epiphanies, psychoanalysis, Zen Buddhism. The twentieth century has built up a powerful set of intellectual shortcuts
and devices that help us defend ourselves against moments when
clouds suddenly appear to think. To say that clouds know something is to sound a little mad. Or, worse, whimsical: It conjures
up the image of a Technicolor *Silly Symphony*, with trees singing
campfire songs accompanied by warbling foxes and rabbits.

But this seems a long way from whimsy: Lavretsky has given
away some of his emotional and intellectual autonomy, and sud-

denly the things surrounding him have their own thoughts and feelings—not necessarily his—and in his reduction of the human scale, Lavretsky's misery disappears. Lavretsky has momentarily recognized an integrity in nature that was invisible as long as he made himself gigantic with pain and problems. Lavretsky's misery will reappear because the plot demands it and because nature can't really solve the sort of problems that Lavretsky has. But this moment will take on its small odd memorability and energy and provide a scale against which to measure the size of Lavretsky's troubles.

In this century, the fiction with which we have grown familiar has tended to insist on the insentience and thoughtlessness of things, if not their outright malevolence. Generally things have no presence at all in stories except as barriers or rewards for human endeavor. When nature is given something like a face to look back at humans, as it often is in Conrad's stories and novels, the expression on that face is typically one of straightforward malice. The violence of nature—its typhoons and malevolent alienness—is what nature tosses back at men who are deeply involved in the project of imperialism. If, as Conrad often insists, imperialism is a kind of rape of nature, then it shouldn't be a surprise that man's violence is visited upon him in return, coming the other way as a force field of unknowingness, the "sullen, dumb, menacing hostility," for example, that Lena perceives in the forest in *Victory*. This often leaves Conrad's characters in a highly specified null-location where the only option is not to grant objects much visibility of any kind. As Winnie Verloc says again and again in *The Secret Agent,* most things do not bear very much looking into.

It's possible, however, that contemporary fiction has gradually been developing a fascinated relationship with objects that parallels in some respects the concerns of various ecological movements. Saying that the realms of objects and humans may be collaborative, however, is obviously risky. It sounds like another form of crackpot New Age dogma, akin to saying that horses understand subatomic physics but can't convey how *much* they know.

Furthermore, human violence against nature has continued as enthusiastically as ever. Forests are being clear-cut and burned, rivers are . . . well, everyone knows the inventory. The human population on the planet continues to increase at an alarming rate. To argue in this context that things may be making visible a correspondence to human feelings still sounds sentimental and weak-minded, at first hearing. What may be good for fiction is not necessarily good in the realm of ideas. I feel that I am trying to justify something in fiction whose truth-claims outside of fiction I'd happily ignore. To talk about sentient trees in stories is to sound crazy or lamebrained; and John Ruskin's concept of the pathetic fallacy is deeply implicated in these two responses, and my own defensiveness.

Madness, like every other spiritual condition, has to be culturally defined. Ruskin thought of himself as just such a definer, a type Gertrude Stein called "a village explainer." It was once the habit of literary critics to create and define fallacies, and Ruskin formulated and delineated the *pathetic fallacy* in 1856. In this essay, Ruskin takes it upon himself to define what he calls an "unhinged" literary response to nature by analyzing certain metaphors that writers employ. What Ruskin asserted as an aesthetic working principle became an informal aesthetic law in the twentieth century. My interest here is not so much to argue against that law as to ask how it came into existence in the first place.

Things, Ruskin says, should not be made to reflect the emotions of the observer. In poetry and prose, human emotions should not be allowed to discolor the integrity of the observed phenomena. Things are not people and they do not have feelings, period. Although Ruskin would not have put it this way, his objection is to an overspillage of human expression onto the things that surround the individual. Ruskin's claim in this chapter of *Modern Painters* that the projection of human feeling on things is fallacious, untrue, morbid, and frightful has all the violence of a Victorian ideology that's meant to put certain kinds of poets in their place. Ruskin is attacking a certain kind of metaphor, used to describe messy feelings. His examples are interesting. One includes two lines from a poem by Oliver Wendell Holmes:

> The spendthrift crocus, bursting through the mold
> Naked and shivering, with his cup of gold.

Curiously enough, Ruskin does not object to "naked and shivering" but to "spendthrift." The crocus, he says, is *not* spendthrift but "hardy." It does not give away its wealth; it hoards. Ruskin finds the poem's metaphor for the plant's economic life mistaken, and, as he says, "untrue." But in eliminating one metaphor for plant life—"spendthrift"—Ruskin substitutes another metaphor—"hardy"—without appearing to recognize that the inescapability of metaphors and figurative language is part of the problem that he thinks he is trying to correct.

Ruskin converts the crocus from an undisciplined squanderer of a fortune into a young Victorian gentleman and banker. Having corrected the poem, he moves on to another example.

This time it is from a novel by Charles Kingsley. Ruskin quotes with considerable distaste the phrase "cruel, crawling foam" and argues that as a phrase it is "unhinged." Foam isn't cruel; it's just foam. This is a clear enough point. When people say that "the storm is raging," as they have for ages, there is no real rage in the storm. The rage is human and is projected upon the storm. Human attributes cross a boundary line and are wrongfully stitched to the nonhuman.

Of course, to say "the storm is raging" is not necessarily expressive. It may be a way of knowing the storm. This habit of knowing is acquired in childhood and not always discarded. "Time is a river" and "life is a dream" are not essentially different formulations, in this respect.

In his entertainingly irascible way, Ruskin is doing his best to define a problem that is considerably larger than he is (Ezra Pound and Robert Bly have repeated his point in subsequent decades). Ruskin is describing the distortion of perceptions that, he believes, occurs when someone has what he calls "violent feelings." Violent feelings, he says, produce a "falseness in all our impressions of external things." Panic, for example, produces metaphors of the type he dislikes. Feelings, or as he says, "souls," can be compared to things, but the separateness of the emotions and the things must be maintained. In his opinion, Dante maintains this distance but Coleridge does not. The result is what Ruskin calls a "morbid" effect in Coleridge. Ruskin is right about the effect but wrong about the cause. The world's integrity can be saved, he believes, through the deployment of a discriminating sensibility and an internally consistent theological system. As we might say now, it's certainly nice to think so.

At certain times of day, Ruskin's respect for sanity is lovable, as is his hope that the worlds of human consciousness and nature can be made figuratively distinct. He is like a man who prefers sunlight to gloom. Behind his anger is a certain understandable squeamishness, a distaste for any kind of aesthetic confusion. He desires clarity. He distrusts the whole project of metaphor.

And there is a sense also behind his words that he is entering a battle that he suspects he is going to lose. Ruskin sees nature being entered, mucked around with, and violated for the purposes of a paltry and second-rate lyricism.

Everywhere Ruskin looks, he sees the human presence expanding. Humanity has become imperial; it's *using* objects to express itself. Poets are shamelessly taking over objects for cheap effects; this is imperialism at the level of aesthetics. Objects are being forced to go to work, carrying lunch pails, putting their shoulders to the wheel—they are being *employed* as a literary workforce to carry their burden of human feeling. No one is leaving objects alone anymore—not in industry, and not in literature, either.

Ruskin wants to stop this expansionism and confusion of realms, but he has to do so by bracketing violent feelings and the atrocities that give rise to them and putting them to the side somewhere. In a rather English manner, he seems to want to deny that when people look at things, things look back. He is thus resisting both emotional violence and the Being that on occasion seems to gaze out from objects. His assumption is that all emotional violence arises out of sensationalism and a carelessness in the notation of the inner life. For him, emotional confusion is by its very nature violent. All this, as I've said, is understandable and even lovable, and it has the sound of someone sitting in a comfortable study and saying that there will be no war, there must not be a war, even as the guns of the twentieth century start blasting away, the new atrocities are revealed, and the terms of the war are announced by the John-the-Baptist of apocalypse, Friedrich Nietzsche.

Ruskin's essay on the pathetic fallacy takes its place in a larger quarrel about the division of literary property in the nineteenth century. At about the time of the rise of the English novel, a marker or borderline begins to appear in literary consciousness that makes the relationship between the inner life of human beings and the inner life of objects almost exclusively a matter for poetry. It is as if all the speaking about the terms of the relationship between people and the spirit within things will occur in poetry and poetics or in almost uncategorizable writing such as theosophy and anthroposophy. We begin to hear about these matters from William Wordsworth and Charles Baudelaire, W. B. Yeats and Vallejo, Madame Blavatsky and Rudolf Steiner, Francis Ponge, and Rainer Maria Rilke.

Rilke's treatment of inanimate objects can be celebratory, as in one of his best-known poems, "Archaic Torso of Apollo,"—in this poem, the statue, though inanimate stone, is filled with more being than the living observer. Eyeless, the statue still sees from every point of its surface. This gives it an overwhelming, uncanny energy. What it contains is immobilized power—the archaic torso is so powerful that it interrogates anyone who sees it. What Rilke loves and is transfixed by is the transfiguring strength of the body in stone and its ability to diminish the mere human presence of anyone who stands before it. Under its stony gaze, every life is insufficient, every life must change. In this respect the torso is like Rilke's famous panther, in Edward Snow's translation, "a dance of strength around a center."

What is more curious is Rilke's hatred of objects without strength, particularly dolls. His essay on dolls, from 1914, coming as it does just before World War I, is itself warlike: Rilke is attacking dolls for their dependency. Rilke dislikes the way children depend on dolls, and he dislikes even more the way dolls depend on humans after the humans have outgrown them: The dolls sit around getting dusty, staring from the corner, wanting something, anything. He finds what he calls "the doll-soul" contemptible. The essay grows quite heated about the deadening and demanding gaze of dolls, their general weakness: Even the other household objects hate dolls, Rilke claims, including tables. This is why we so often find dolls on the floor, where the stronger objects have flung them.

For Rilke the archaic torso is not an object so much as a living stone, a being, because his imagination is energized and productively destabilized by it. The torso collaborates in the poem about it. But the dolls really *are* objects, and they remain objects, stuff-with-bad-souls, because they cringingly ask for some response from his imagination that Rilke, in his pride, refuses to give them. Accordingly, the dolls appear in an essay, not a poem. All they deserve is prose. They are dead but refuse to leave the poet alone. He doesn't like their hideous sweetness, their mute cries for assistance. They don't take him anywhere. They're like babies, Rilke observes, messing themselves with play food. And there is nothing less transcendent than a baby at mealtime or afterwards. This is the side of Rilke that is non-parental and Nietzschean and power fixated, that wants to be overmastered by huge spiritual flood tides, that distrusts family life, that has a queasy contempt for nurturing, that sees all the forms of domestic daily existence as mewling and antipoetical.

Rilke's struggles with his subjects and objects are so fierce and mind haunting that the only means of getting completely free of his influence is to write prose fiction. As it happens, Rilke's division of subjects, some into prose, the more nobler ones into poetry, replicates a division that was already underway in the last decades of the nineteenth century.

By the late nineteenth century, it is as if the division of realms, as in a bad divorce settlement, had become absolute, with no conversation between the two parties: Poetry was supposed to get the spirit, and fiction got the material world. Poetry, particularly in France, laid claim to its airy realm by turning to symbolism, and fiction got down into its particularized mud with naturalism and the relentless object-catalogues of Zola and Dreiser. The stages of this process are all outlined by the Spanish journalist and philosopher José Ortega y Gasset in his wonderfully barbed *Meditations on Quixote*. Don Quixote, he says, is the spirit of epic poetry who hears all things speaking. Sancho Panza is the practical materialist, the spirit of the rise of the novel. Cervantes' novel is the thunderous and comic announcement that Don Quixote is about to be supplanted in human history by Sancho Panza. Narrative epic poetry, displaced by narrative prose, turns into pure lyric, which can keep its heroism and its madness (and its sacred speaking objects and its absolutist transcendental power), but prose from now on will be delegated to speak about material life. However, there's a catch: The material will all be quite dead. Poetry gets the spirit and hears it speak but is called mad. Prose fiction is given a landscape of dead objects and is rewarded for writing about these things with a popular acclaim, a mass audience. This is a particularly solipsistic and Puritan solution to the problem of inner and outer worlds.

Following this model, one can understand why, when Don Quixote is dying and has regained his lucidity, Sancho Panza wants him to be his old self again: heroic and mad and epical. Living by himself, Sancho is going to be stuck with a paunch and a world of mute things. So much the worse for him, but he *has* survived, in the way that laboratory science has survived its unruly spirit-obsessed parent, alchemy, and for some of the same reasons. Marxism survives Hegelianism until something turns up to displace dialectical materialism. Everyone remembers Sancho Panza's tears at the deathbed of Don Quixote. Materialism without ideals, mad or not, weeps. Deprived of a quest, it is consigned to centuries of weeping.

People in a traumatized state tend to love their furniture. They become ferociously attached to knickknacks. Laura and her love for her glass menagerie in Tennessee Williams's play will have to stand for a whole platoon of the dispossessed for whom objects have come alive. To write about such spiritual conditions, an author might do better to describe the furniture as a character sees it than to describe the consciousness of the person entering the room. How a person sees the things that surround him usually tells us more than an explicit description of his mood. The things carry the feeling. They do not when our emotions are placid, but when our emotions are violent, they must.

In an age of violent emotions, objects become as expressive as the people who live among them. They take on a weird, uncanny life, the life of a fetish. I think of Daisy Buchanan here, getting into a weepy state over Gatsby's shirts. Objects in that book reward the careless hysteria with which they're treated by gazing back, smoldering in waste piles, and then running down innocent bystanders. There is a subtle anthropomorphism on almost every page of *The Great Gatsby,* as befits a novel about idolatry and consumerism. But Anglo-American fiction, unlike poetry, has been slow to arrive at the sort of interplay between things and people that Fitzgerald's novel claims as its subject. It wants to contain objects and material but to give all the feelings to the human characters. Objects in *Gatsby* are invested with tremendous feeling, and it's sometimes hard to tell what the source of that feeling is. The curtains and the ashtrays and the billboards in this novel sometimes seem more alive than the characters surrounding them (also true of the French *nouveau roman,* the so-called new novel).

My intention in the remainder of this essay is to single out certain passages of fiction where objects rather than people (or objects in conjunction with people) are expressive or even sentient, and thus become characters. In this way, objects become subjects. These examples risk the appearance of whimsy and lunacy, as I've said, but only because they're written in prose. According to the terms of the divorce, sentient objects can appear in poetry such as Rilke's, but not in fiction. The blunt materialistic common sense of fiction is supposed to resist this reconciliation. But it doesn't, anymore, if it ever did.

The middle section of *To the Lighthouse,* "Time Passes," is a good place to start. In my experience, many readers skip over this section, aghast, as if it were a literary externalization of one of Virginia Woolf's manic fits. In a certain light, these pages can seem both fey and bizarre, not so much childlike as childish. Woolf herself made a great point in her essays and polemics about wanting to reincorporate material objects in fiction with what she called a "luminous halo," and this section feels like the revenge of the luminous halo on the stuff of the material world. Her quarrel with the novels of Arnold Bennett had to do with the manner in which objects appeared in fiction. She concluded that Bennett was a crude materialist and that this produced in his novels an offensive man-of-the-world knowingness about worldly things. Against this, she proposes a kind of spiritualization of the world of objects, which, at its extreme point, swings the wand of the Sorcerer's Apprentice over the summer house and breathes life into objects, moving them into a world halfway between ours and theirs.

This is probably not a satisfactory solution to the rise of an industrial economy committed to the prodigious slaughters of World War I. But then, where *are* the satisfactory solutions? Nobody in the novel or outside of it can claim to know what those solutions might have been or might be. In this context, Virginia Woolf's writerly efforts in *To the Lighthouse* can seem positively heroic.

There are really two locales of magic in "Time Passes": One is the black magic of arbitrary death and trench warfare in World War I, and the other is the writerly imaginative magic applied to the Ramsay house. The black magic of the war is now known by everyone and, despite the piles of corpses, has lost its power to shock. Against this maniac pan-European killing spree, Virginia Woolf gives us by contrast . . . a summer house.

The main character in the section is the Ramsay place, vacated by the Ramsays, as it gradually loses its integrity and form. The house-as-soul is a convenient and ancient emblem and probably applies here. The other two actors in this section are darkness and wind. Human beings are, in this section, secondary to objects and spirits. There is a cleaning woman, Mrs. McNab, and her helper, Mrs. Bast, both of whom appear late in the section to clean things up, but when the members of the Ramsay family are mentioned, their names and their actions appear within brackets.

Death, violent or sudden, is held within these brackets. Mrs. Ramsay dies suddenly from an unnamed illness. Prue Ramsay dies in childbirth. Andrew Ramsay is killed in the war. These calamities are narrated with a weirdly disturbing offhandedness. It's like your maiden aunt telling you, with a vague impassive expression, during tea, that the elementary school down the street was dynamited last week and several children were killed, including your cousin. The narrative consciousness of *To the Lighthouse* refuses to dwell on these deaths. They are the stuff of trauma, and in the world of this novel they are nonnarratable. Beyond stating the bare facts, trauma cannot speak of itself. If it could, it wouldn't be trauma. The odd purity of true suffering, in this case, is that it *demonstrates* nothing. The facts manage to be the sufficient shock. Any narrative inflation of pain, any demonstration of it, is exploitative, and a betrayal.

In this novel the death of the spirit cannot be housed

narratively in the flesh where that death occurs but must move
into the dwelling place of the body, the house itself. When a
writer can't resurrect the body, she can at least resurrect the
place where the body lived.

As a result, what happens in this section tonally has a touch
of fable, horror movie, and children's story. In passages such as
the following I hear a voice almost unknown to the Modernist
novel:

> Only through the rusty hinges and swollen sea-moistened
> woodwork certain airs, detached from the body of the wind
> (the house was ramshackle after all) crept round corners and
> ventured indoors. Almost one might imagine them, as they
> entered the drawing-room questing and wondering, toying
> with the flap of hanging wall-paper, asking, would it hang
> much longer, would it fall?

I recognize this voice. It says, "Now listen, children." At some
outer limit of pain, innocence is being allowed to enter through
a back door, a secret entrance. A diversion is being staged, possibly to plague and confound worldliness and sophistication.

Abstract qualities in this section are given human form at
the same time that humans lose it:

> Loveliness and stillness clasped hands in the bedroom, and
> among the shrouded jugs and sheeted chairs even the prying
> of the wind, and the soft nose of the clammy sea airs, rubbing,
> snuffling, iterating, and reiterating their questions—"Will
> you fade? Will you perish?"—scarcely disturbed the peace, the
> indifference, the air of pure integrity, as if the question they
> asked scarcely needed that they should answer: we remain.

As the members of the family die, the house is invaded by
wind and rain and darkness. We witness a soul, a house, a house-
as-soul, dying also. The feeling in these passages is peculiar,

beautifully peculiar, at least to my ear, but there's also a quality of lyric terror. Some people who go off into this particular world never come back. They get cloyed to it. Anyone can see the risk. It's as if the mice and the saucepans have been enlisted to stand against the other war, as subjects: If this is whimsy, it's become almost metaphysical. As saucepans rust, the mats decay, and the toads invade the interior, and as the lighthouse watches "with equanimity" while the house is undermined, all forms of the pathetic fallacy are put on display.

But what is being projected onto the house is not a human feeling, but a god's. Spirits give life, but in this case they also rot. The spirit world has its share of demons. The tone of the sentences mixes wonderment with incantation, as if magic circles were being created. You recognize this tone in children's literature, but you don't expect to find it in English novels until you think about the ambivalence toward worldly power Virginia Woolf's novels usually display. This leap to childhood may be regressive, but its desperation lends it an air of audacity. Some ancient source of wonder is being cracked at its origin so that life, some life, might be sustained. If humans are to suffer spirit-death, things will too. By this method the "something" that lies behind our objects will be glimpsed:

> But there was a force working; something not highly conscious; something that leered, something that lurched; something not inspired to go about its work with dignified ritual or solemn chanting.

"Solemn chanting" is a fairly good description of the method of "Time Passes." This "something" has to be tricked out of hiding. Solemn chanting may just do it, along with fable, lyric, and whimsy—all the discarded techniques of the English novel. The "something" spied in this passage is not malignant, but it does not gaze with equanimity, either, as the lighthouse does. It is a dead spirit being brought back to life in the revival of things in which it can find habitation. As the house is restored, so is the presence that lies behind it.

Using a voice invoking magic, this section of Woolf's novel equates housekeeping with religion. Taking care of things, it claims, is the way back to the reconstitution of the spirit. It gives a sentience to objects as the containers of that spirit. It declares a truce between humans and objects, and it observes that if any group effects the repair, it will probably be women, women who have never read Descartes, who would not understand Descartes if they did read him. Against the absolute separation of man and thing, the mind-body dichotomy tormenting Mr. Ramsay, the novel proposes a therapeutic incomprehension, a profitable forgetting. Innocence, which no one ever gets back, *is* recovered here by sheer force of manic willpower.

The solemn and lyrical zaniness of "Time Passes," its cast of characters of rats, frogs, wind, darkness, and spirit makes it immune to skepticism. The writing doesn't carry on a conversation with skepticism. It can't. The entire section is enclosed in a sort of time-bubble, where it speaks only to itself and is overheard by the reader. The person who asks, "How do you *know* that loveliness and stillness clasped hands in the bedroom?" is off in another world, the world of Mr. Ramsay, in parts one and three of *To the Lighthouse,* where such questions have a footing. They don't here. A context has been established that repels the grindstones of reason.

In *To the Lighthouse* the reconciliation of matter and spirit is managed at such a high level of psychic virtuosity that you hold your breath while reading it. Aesthetically, it almost does not happen, in the same way that James Ramsay is almost not reconciled to his father as they sail out to the lighthouse in the closing pages of the book. James wants to kill his father, knife him for his emotional coldness and his other crimes against the spirit. But the wind fills the sails at the last moment, Mr. Ramsay says, "Well done!" and James "was so pleased that he was not going to let anyone share a grain of his pleasure." Opportunistic violence is bracketed at last and removed from the scene of narrative.

The fragility of these narrative instances can hardly be over-stated. I do not find anything much like it, certainly in American writing, for another two decades, although traces of it turn up in Elizabeth Bowen's novels. What happens instead is a narrative interest in the anger of objects, the fierce hostility of things to man and his enterprises. (This is also mixed up with the gradual conversion in some literature during the same historical period of human beings into things such as robots or clockworks or androids. But that would be the subject of another essay.)

Thomas Pynchon's Byron the Bulb in *Gravity's Rainbow* travels from bulb babyhood to a tour of the world's systemic cartels, including the light cartel, Phoebus. In Pynchon's encapsulated lightbulb bildungsroman, Byron, who is immortal, sees the truth of the human systems but "is condemned to go on forever, knowing the truth and powerless to change anything. No longer will he seek to get off the wheel. His anger and frustration will grow without limit, and he will find himself, poor perverse bulb, enjoying it. . . ."

As in much of Pynchon, this Olympian understanding leads to immobilized rage and hysterical comedy. It is now power rather than capital that moves in a tidal ebb and flow. The more you understand about the system, the more immobilized you are. *This* Byronism is masochistic but does not lead to a revolt of the objects against their masters. It just grows in helpless raging understanding. Anger and frustration expand to fill any space available to house them.

These two novels, Pynchon's and Woolf's, are both in their way about warfare and the violation of the earth. When greed, violence, and the various other human vices begin to make the home planet unhomelike—in German, *unheimlich*—the uncanny erupts out of things that were silent. Objects are forced to speak, to become visible when the home is endangered. The double meaning of *unheimlich* as both *unhomelike* and *uncanny* is a traditional puzzle. Freud worried over it in his "On the Uncanny" and saw it, in part, as the estrangement of the familiar.

The estrangement of the familiar: One of its forms is soul-theft. This tradition is very strong in Russian literature and finds its great artist in Nikolai Gogol, whose work tracks and shadows the soul as it is bought and sold, and in whose work objects seem to be living a giddy life of their own. Leo Tolstoy, too: In the first section of "The Death of Ivan Ilych," Pavel Ivanovich suffers the pranksterish rebellious springs of the chair he sits on, while Praskovya Fedorovna, the grieving widow, gets her shawl stuck on the side of a table. These are not accidents: The objects want it that way, in Tolstoy's reckoning. Loveless petty functionaries in this story come face-to-face with the perversity of inanimate objects, beginning with their sickening bodies and going on from there. The trading and buying of souls enlivens the uncanny in Mikhail Bulgakov and Vladimir Nabokov as well. In Nabokov's *Bend Sinister,* located in a police state, the dictator Paduk is doing his best to acquire the soul of the philosopher Adam Krug. Krug's friends, the little things, haplessly sing tunes to him he can only half see and half hear.

> The stove crackled gently, and a square clock with two corn-flowers painted on its white wooden face and no glass rapped out the seconds in pica type. The window attempted a smile. A faint infusion of sunshine spread over the distant hill and brought out with a kind of pointless distinction the little

farm and three pine trees on the opposite slope which seemed to move forward and then to retreat again as the wan sun swooned.

If this is the pathetic fallacy, whose pathos is it? Where is the fallacy? Modes of thought are fallacious as long as we are not being tortured, but in a state of extreme emotion, when objects really begin to speak, the categories of "false" and "true" no longer make the same kind of sense. The floating perceptions in this passage have a detachment so complete they have a feeling of weightlessness in an enclosure defined by suffering. In this sense they possess the suspended feeling of "Time Passes," a vehement and insistent innocence.

The word "setting," especially as it is used in fiction-writing textbooks and workshops, has a drab, dutiful quality. Setting is the element in fiction that seems the least susceptible to imaginative work. It's already there, always. Put it in the foreground and you get snide compliments about local color. The usual assumption is that setting is objective, that it "helps" and "shapes" a story. In the way that I am describing them, however, the objects and things surrounding fictional characters have the same status *and energy* as the characters themselves. Setting—in the way I want to define it—is not just a place where action occurs. (Nor is the Earth just a prized location where our lives happen to happen. This planet is not just a setting for us, laid out for our benefit.)

Setting projects a mode of feeling that corresponds to—or contrasts with—the action. The way that setting is usually taught in fiction-writing classes results in the fictional equivalent of a curtain rising on a stage set with one desk, one potted plant, and a stairway reaching toward empty air. It is background rather than foreground. What surrounds the characters, however, *can* be as expressive as the action. No law dictates that the setting should always express the feelings of the characters. Too often, however, it does. Call it *the fallacy of the objective correlative,* the setting that can only express the feelings of the characters. A sad man sees sad trees. A murderous man gazes upon a murderous lake.

This kind of one-to-one equivalency makes John Ruskin's ideas about the pathetic fallacy seem sensible all over again. If objects reflect only the characters who look upon them, they have nothing to tell us. All they would do is mirror us. They would enlarge, once again, the human realm. But the human realm in our time needs no further enlargement. It is already bloated, in many senses at once. If a mountain exists only to express or reflect human feelings about it or anything else, it is diminished, so that humans can be its conquerors. It isn't only species that are endangered in our time; so is scale, a feeling for immensity. When that happens, phrases like "the sublime" lose all their force. They become comic and pretentious.

Examples of mute objects in fiction are so common that despite their number they can't even ask for our attention; but the speaking of objects over the heads of characters directly to readers is so beautifully managed in William Maxwell's writing from the last fifty years that it makes one think of Virginia Woolf, transported to the American Midwest. Modesty, and a variety of wonder that is never naïve, replace the usual forms of worldliness and willfulness in *this* fiction, which is often set in Illinois and located at a particular time, often the 1920s and 1930s, although in Maxwell's more recent work we are brought into our own time. Maxwell's fiction habitually loves its characters, festoons them with intricate details, mostly, I think, because the world that surrounds them is typically fearful and subject to violent change. His stories are transparently about home—where home is, what it is, and what makes it canny or uncanny. Most of Maxwell's characters, in his first four novels, are fated to fall in love with the wrong person or to find themselves ejected from home. That is what drives his plots and what gives them their characteristic eeriness.

In his 1948 novel *Time Will Darken It,* for example, Nora Potter, the young woman who will fall in love with a married man, Austin King, finds herself located at the center of what would be in other respects a conventional narrative—if the town where it occurs, Draperville, Illinois, were not so articulate. But in this novel, because everything is loved, everything speaks. The "mindless, kindless voice of nature," as the narrator calls it, utters its thoughts through the heat, the locusts, the rain, and the bric-a-brac. Addressed only to the reader, it bypasses the characters, who are unaware of it. One example from many will have to suffice:

> The house was so still that it gave her the feeling that she was being watched, that the sofas and chairs were keeping an eye on her to see that she didn't touch anything that she shouldn't; that she put back the alabaster model of the Taj Mahal and the little bearded grinning man (made out of ivory, with a pack on his back, a folded fan, and his toes turned inward) exactly the way she found them. The locusts warned her, but from too far away. The clocks all seemed preoccupied with their various and contradictory versions of the correct time.

This passage begins with Nora's feelings, but it has more feelings than Nora can reasonably carry, and by the time the paragraph is over, Nora is insufficient to explain them. She has been diminished just enough so that the locusts can speak without being heard by her. It's one of those stories that has more intricate emotions than the characters themselves do. The passage notices that the little bearded man made out of ivory has toes turned inward, but it is unclear whether Nora notices that. Here, she is one thing in a field of things. And she is about to violate those things in a dreamy obtuse way. If we have caught the feeling of the scene, we probably know that Nora is going to suffer eventually, that things (in this case, in the form of fire) will have their revenge for her interference.

In his tender and antiheroic fiction, Maxwell lovingly puts his characters in their places. Like Turgenev's Lavretsky and like Chekhov's characters, they slowly learn what it means to have a sense of scale. In the only way that matters, they are humbled by being placed in proximity to objects that, quoting the Turgenev translation again, "seem to know where they were going."

When humans are oblivious and oppressed to the point of madness, objects take on the humanity that humans lack. In Cynthia Ozick's "The Shawl," a story about a concentration camp, the shawl takes on the burden of nurturing Magda, a malnourished infant, and becomes a breast and a womb and a house. The electric fencing around the death camp, as if disturbed by the role it plays, hums with "grainy sad voices." In Tim O'Brien's "The Things They Carried," the American soldiers in Vietnam transfer all their feelings to the objects they "hump," as the narrative has it: Feeling, dispossessed by humans, moves quickly into the nearest receptacle willing to house it. The more one looks for enlivened objects in contemporary literature, the more visible they become—in Bruno Schulz, or Patrick White, or Bessie Head. We would expect to find it in the literature of Africa, where it is common to believe that if you build anything by hand, such as a table, the table will contain some small part of your soul. And not metaphorically, either.

My stepfather liked on winter weekends to repair broken furniture, and he often gave me the responsibility of holding his tools while he did the work. Because he was a man of small patience and terrible temper, but with a high vision of himself, he would turn screws or hammer nails with a bland expression on his face that revealed almost nothing. Only his skin revealed his feelings: It grew redder and redder as his fury against inanimate objects increased. Holding his tools, I thought: He's a steam engine, and he's going to explode any minute now.

He never cursed and hardly spoke while doing these tasks. He took himself, as an upper-class, lapsed Protestant, very seriously. But when he exhaled, he exhaled through his nose in regular three-second intervals, exhalations of the purest rage, utterly machinelike, so much so that I cannot now hear the distant sound of a stamping plant or a production line without thinking of my stepfather. Holding his tools, I felt sorry for the screws and nails. They screamed and squeaked as they fell under my stepfather's attention.

During the time I worked on this essay, I tried to explain its subject to my wife and son, at dinner. My son, who was fifteen, let it be known that he did not understand what I was talking about and when he did understand it, he didn't like it and thought I had gone off the deep end. "'The inner life of objects'?" he'd ask. "Is that like . . . uh, talking forks?" And I'd say, "Yes, that is what it's like. Those odd moments when things seem to say something." "*What* odd moments?" he'd ask.

Outside the window is an apple tree. It is August as I write these sentences. For the last few days a squirrel has been foraging in the tree, and sometimes it descends low enough on one of the branches in front of my study window to take a good look at me. It can stare at me for two minutes without moving. Then it goes back to its business, as I do to mine.

We do not spray the tree, and the apples growing there are mostly green or wormy. During the time that I have been writing this essay, the apples have been falling to the ground in the backyard. Every now and then, writing a sentence, I have heard the sound of an apple hitting the earth. Before the sound of that impact, there is a breath, a swish, as the fruit drops through the branches and leaves. It is not a sigh but sounds like one. This sound has nothing to do with my current moods, but I listen for it, and I have been counting the number of apples that have fallen during the last ten pages of this essay. There have been eighteen.

Notes

Sigmund Freud, "The Uncanny," in *On Creativity and the Unconscious.* Edited by Benjamin Nelson (New York: Harper and Row, 1958): 122–161.

Alvin Greenberg, "The Revolt of Objects: The Opposing World in the Modern Novel," *Centennial Review* 13:4 (Fall 1969): 366–388.

Rainer Maria Rilke, "Some Reflections on Dolls," in *Where Silence Reigns: Selected Prose.* Translated by G. Craig Houston (New York: New Directions, 1978): 43–50.

Counterpointed Characterization

It's evening, summer, a party out on the back lawn, but most of the guests have left. A few of them are still sitting out there, listlessly slapping at mosquitoes and watching, with a kind of tired curiosity, the occasional green flares of the fireflies. I've gone inside for another beer and stand at the kitchen window, listening. I'm spying on my own party. They're talking about a friend we all know whose life, through a series of romantic miscalculations, has become a story. There is an ex-wife, a girl-friend, children, an episode with a rowboat, and confusion. Not so extraordinary a story, when you think about it, but one worth telling for its little irritating granules of truth and pain. I hold my beer, the cold aluminum inside my palm, and I wonder: Do they ever talk about me that way? When they drive home from the party, the one my wife and I have put together for them, do they talk about us? To whom do we get compared?

Gossip invites all sorts of comparison-contrast. That man over there, Gus, is a sleaze; and we convince ourselves that he *is* a sleaze because at the same moment we can manage to conjure up his cousin Burt, the boring moral paragon. My friends sitting out on the backyard, slapping at mosquitoes (why didn't we spray? where are the citronella candles?) think of the seemingly disastrous life of our friend, comparing it to their own. *He's not us, at least not yet.* But we are like Ivan Ilych's friends who, upon hearing of his death, think: Well, at least it wasn't me. We seem to know ourselves, socially at least, only by comparing ourselves to someone else, to others. We knit together what comparative context we can.

In day-to-day life we play these little games of comparison-contrast in which we are usually the contrast. I wouldn't have done it that way. I wouldn't have done that at all. Look at him, now, the one who did it, sinking. *At least it wasn't me!* By telling stories in this manner, we become narratable. We find a story for ourselves. We spin around ourselves, in what seems to be a natural form, the cobweb of a plot. We move our own lives into the condition of narrative progression. Plot often develops out of the tensions between characters, and in order to get that tension, a writer sometimes has to be a bit of a matchmaker, creating characters who counterpoint one another in ways that are fit for gossip. Our hapless friend is a character, but not yet *my* character. With counterpointed characterization, certain kinds of people are pushed together, people who bring out a crucial response to each other. A latent energy rises to the surface, the desire or secret previously forced down into psychic obscurity.

It seems to be in the nature of plots to bring a truth or a desire up to the light, and it has often been the task of those who write fiction to expose elements that are kept secret in a personality, so that the mask over that personality (or any system) falls either temporarily or permanently. When the mask falls, something of value comes up. Masks are interesting partly for themselves and partly for *what* they mask. The reality behind the mask is like a shadow-creature rising to the bait: the tug of an unseen force, frightening and energetic. What emerges is a precious thing, precious because buried or lost or repressed.

Anyone who writes stories or novels or poems with some kind of narrative structure often imagines a central character, then gives that character a desire or a fear and perhaps some kind of goal and sets another character in a collision course with that person. The protagonist collides with an antagonist. All right: We know where we are. We often talk about this sort of dramatic conflict as if it were all unitary, all of one kind: One person wants something, another person wants something else, and conflict results. But this is not, I think, the way most stories actually work. Not everything is a contest. We are not always fighting our brothers for our share of the worldly goods. Many good stories have no antagonist at all. My friends on the lawn don't tell their stories that way. Actual conflict can be a fairly minor element in most stories, written or told. A more appropriate question might be, "What's emerging here?" or: "What's showing up?"

The family has been the scene for many of these counterpoint narratives. It is hard to talk about the family these days as a subject of fiction without feeling the presence of contemporary reactionary politics. These movements have done their best to co-opt the family and to turn it into a kind of kitsch social unit.

The concept of "family values" is inherently rigid and inflexible. It's meant to stop thought. Good fiction and theater usually assume that "family values" should be in some kind of interesting uproar. To remove contrast from within the family and to substitute an idea of uniformity is to kill off art for political ends. The family becomes a small molecular army, on the march for rectitude. Political representations of "family values" thus have a quality of poster art, and because they have a relationship to propaganda, they are nearly always tainted by a feeling of false surfaces. In other words, they have a mean-spirited wish to be endearing and cute. The result is a sort of nostalgia lacquered with rage, characteristic of the art of police states.

But the family as a subject has given tremendous energy to the novel and to theater, and that energy has often arisen from counterpointed or incompatible family values. Even *Ulysses* is a novel, at least in part, about family values, although the family values in this novel are not notably exemplary. It is pleasing and relaxing to imagine a right-wing politician trying to turn the marriage of Leopold and Molly Bloom to political ends.

Stories often arise when two characters who hardly belong together are forced to inhabit the same frame of reference, as they often must in families. Alice Walker's story "Everyday Use" contains two sisters, the lovable and slow-witted Maggie, who has never left home, and her brilliant sister, Dee, who is frighteningly articulate and beautiful and a sort of *arriviste* Afrocentric. Also, she has a mean streak. Dee frightens even her mother, who tells the story of Dee's most recent homecoming. Dee looks around at the quilts and the butter churn and the other household items, and, like the middle-class social climber she is, imagines them as decorative pieces, suitable for display. During her time away from home, Dee has become an anthropologist of her own family's life. She wants to hang the family quilts on the walls. Maggie wants them for everyday use. Their mother, the narrator, must choose between them.

The first time I read Alice Walker's story, I thought: Well, this isn't conflict so much as counterpoint. The whole idea of "conflict" is too unnuanced and newspaperish to apply to this particular tale. Dee and Maggie can hardly inhabit the same stage, but they have to because they're sisters, and the story is arranged so that their mother, of all people, must choose between them. Parents aren't supposed to make such choices, but when they're compelled to, as they usually are sooner or later, it's a story. It doesn't work to say that any one of the three women is a protagonist, or that any one of them is an antagonist. They are subjects and countersubjects, drab authenticity facing down brilliant display. (It's a stacked deck, of course: It's Cinderella and the wicked stepsister, with the fairy godmother telling the tale. The neatness of this makes "Everyday Use" a common anthology piece.)

In narratives like Alice Walker's, counterpointing substitutes for conflict, or displaces it. Parables do this, and stories told for some moral illumination. In parables and children's fables we encounter the sort of tale that begins, "There were two brothers, and one was generous, and one was as mean as a stick." Or: "There was a man with a vineyard, and he had three children." Such stories feel absolutely secure. We know what they mean: Their meaning, their lesson, is already half visible, just off to the side. The contrast itself contains a kind of didacticism. We're about to see people compared. In both cases, the future, in the form of consequences, will materialize quickly. Knowing the future allows the reader to see a moral. All moralizing implies some knowledge of the future.

Call it fate, or call it arrangement, but in stories of counterpointed character I often have the sense of unseen hands pushing people together for narrative purposes. "There was a poor woman, whose husband had died, and she had two daughters." (A reduction of Marilynne Robinson's *Housekeeping*.) "One daughter was practical and conventional, and one was dreamy and vague." Ruth—in that novel—isn't particularly conscious of her contrast to her sister, Lucille, but we are. Also, we can see how she is warped in the direction of her aunt Sylvie. That's the story, which itself is only a meager part of the novel's literary claim upon our attention.

Your contrast to everybody else is the story of your own life that you never realize until it's too late to change it. By the time you realize you're a contrast to someone, you've thrown your allegiance in one direction or the other, toward love or hatred, friendship or subversion. Intelligence is almost no help here. Every time you meet someone, you have the encounter at eye level, ground level. Perhaps sociopaths always have an agenda, a way to put people to use immediately, a bird's-eye view of each and every meeting, but most of the time we don't see people— how could we?—in their entirety. We can't see how we compare to them. Desire of one kind or another usually gets in the way.

Literature, however, is not written at ground level. No encounter in a story ever feels completely naïve or accidental. Literature is arranged. When we read, we are always gazing down at the characters on the page from an angle just slightly above them. We're in possession of what they don't have: their future. We're outside their frame. We hold it in our hands. They're inside the model and we're outside of it. It gives us an edge, and this edge invites a certain kind of superiority, a freedom to make value judgments, to sit out on the lawn and to say that Emma Bovary is making a damn fool of herself.

This difference between being *in* an experience and being slightly *above* it accounts for the fascination that long-term couples have for talking about how they met. Gestures or actions that seemingly had no significance—a spill of wine, a dumb joke—have become bloated with significance because of what subsequently happened. Ask any couple how they met and you will invariably get a story, sometimes told with pleasure, sometimes not, but always a story whose little details are freighted with significance. Because of that ballpoint pen, or that fender bender, or that lost theater ticket: Well, here we are. That's how we met.

The way in which we counterpoint characters tells us about ourselves as matchmakers, and about the characters in relation to each other. Straightforward contrast makes the matchmaker and the match itself seem rather simple. This type of contrast is characteristic, it seems to me, of parables and children's stories and jokes. All three types of stories have a quality of ritual telling. In them, characters are completely subordinated to plot function. A rabbi, a priest, and a Buddhist monk are sitting in a lifeboat, etc. Sometimes this simplification is used to teach a lesson. "Look at X, who turns in her homework *on time*! And look at *you*!"

Fortunately, it's not always so simple. Suppose you have a character who is a shabby genteel Southern lady who has fantasies of lost aristocracy and vague ideas of beauty and tenderness. You have thought of someone vaguely like Blanche Dubois. Now think of her opposite, in almost all respects: A man who works with his hands, very sexual and very ethnic, a sort of crafty survivor with shrewd insights and a bad temper. There stands Stanley Kowalski.

A Streetcar Named Desire, despite its contrasts, doesn't feel like a parable or a joke. It's not even "about" Blanche or Stanley or Stella. It's about what happens when you put them together. In the violence of that meeting, a half-comic and half-tragic incongruity arises. If you have Blanche and Stanley onstage together, you almost don't have to worry about the story. The story will take care of itself. A third element is born when those characters meet. This element is not just drama, the force of conflicting desires. It is a kind of invisible presence whose identity is generated by the proximity of the three characters, and this presence is not moral or simple. If we could state it, we would not need the play. (Gertrude Stein shrewdly remarks that the reason people still talk about *Hamlet* has to do, not with what people understand about it, but with what they continue, down through the years, not to understand.)

Or *King Lear*: In putting Lear's opening public-address pomposity next to Goneril and Regan's pay-per-view eloquence and Cordelia's muteness, we have, generated right in front of us, a theme that involves literal and metaphorical blindness and deafness. Lear's ignorance, full of kinetic potential, generates a landscape of storms, cliffs, and waste. There are lessons here, if anybody wants them—love is often unable to speak, and if you renounce your worldly power and turn the other cheek, you should expect to be slapped a second time—but Lear is a slow learner. Having learned his lessons much too late, he runs out of time. Time has run out for almost everyone else in the play as well except the Duke of Albany, who proves in his last lines that he has figured out at least something from this quasi-parable. *There was a king, accompanied by a fool, and he had three daughters.*

From the counterpointing of the daughters is generated the moral contrast and poetry of the play, so hated by Tolstoy that he wrote an essay attacking everything about it. Tolstoy, Lear. Comparison, contrast.

One kind of counterpoint does not make its way into gossip. My sense of this variety of counterpointed characterization is that it is generated from envy and lodges in the mind when we argue against ourselves. The contrast of the shadow-self involves a secondary character who enacts what we have merely wished for, who is formed by the desires we have never done anything about. In the literature of the shadow-self, some characters throw off a shadow, and the shadow has to do with neediness. Someone wants to do something, but can't, so someone else does it for him, as Ignatius Gallagher does everything that Little Chandler thinks of doing in Joyce's "A Little Cloud."

Stories constructed this way often take place in the dark. Repression blots out the sun, and Victor Frankenstein collects body parts at night and stitches together his impulsive creature at night, usually the only time when the damned thing will talk. We meet ourselves walking toward us on the path at night (Poe, Hawthorne), and the true darknesses we have repressed come leaping out at us with severe intentions (Guitar/Milkman Dead in Toni Morrison's *Song of Solomon*.) In this literature, if any event happens one time, it will probably happen again, but with all its unsavory wishes visible. James M. Cain is a great purveyor of such tales: It's a fiction of seeing double, of getting what you want *at exactly the wrong time.*

The shadow-self is usually, because of the unruly strength of its desires, in a minority and of a minority and has been put to wonderfully wicked use by minority writers of every kind, who, shadowed themselves, speak up exactly for what has been blotted out.

Not everything gets soaked into the blotter, and often in mainstream fiction two characters are set next to each other with the result that neither one wins or loses the moral contest. In some sense, in parallel counterpoint, there is *no* contest. Is Mrs. Ramsey, in *To the Lighthouse,* clearly superior to her husband? Critics and amateur readers have had a tendency to choose sides in this matter, but since the characters are different from, rather than better than, each other, the apples and oranges somehow stay in separate bins. Pick your favorite character in *Ulysses* and then try to establish his/her moral superiority to anyone else in the book. It's a loser's game. We are sometimes teased into it (what are we supposed to think of Charlie Citrine in relation to

Humboldt in *Humboldt's Gift*? The counterpoint in that book is played extravagantly and relentlessly, with the result that moral certainty leaks out of the book page by page, drop by drop). This sort of fiction is neither parable nor night story. Characters are moved together spatially or thematically; they give off light by being in proximity to each other, and then they part.

The variety of possible counterpoints can make a person daydream. There's the story of psychic trade-offs: One person's soul waxes while the other wanes. Or one grows up while the other grows down. The boss becomes the servant. We are in the world of *Tender Is the Night,* of Janet Kauffman's *Collaborators,* and almost anything by Harold Pinter. Another kind of counterpoint employs an inquisitor and a concealer. One character tries to help (or get at) another character in order to make the mask fall for therapeutic or semidemonic reasons, to let the angels or the furies loose. The inquisitor arrives and asks what your life has been about, and you have no choice, you are forced to answer. Eugene O'Neill, Kafka, Christa Wolf, Gogol, Dostoyevsky, Tolstoy. This is a form much loved in central Europe and in Asia, where citizens believe that they must be answerable to someone or something. Here in America, we tend to assume that such questions are no one's goddamn business but our own.

The distrust that many Americans harbor for any community except the family has helped to make us a nation of politically misallied misfits. Misfits don't want to join political parties or fall in love. They want to light out for the territories, proclaim their belief in purity, acquire some firepower, and stay clean. They think of themselves as heroic. The quest is secondary and often incoherent and unintelligible. It is undertaken in a condition of cheerfulness—think of the recent crazed-rictus candidacies of Ross Perot or Steve Forbes. Cheerfulness, as Robert

Bly has argued, is a deeply Puritan emotion, frozen and static, as opposed to joy, which is transfigurative. America, as visitors never tire of pointing out, is full of vaguely sinister cheerfulness. Your murderers smile at you when they shoot you. Robert DeNiro caught this quality in his performance in *Taxi Driver*: The crazier Travis Bickle gets, the more he grins.

Which is why, I think, it's often fictionally interesting to get strangers together in America and start them talking, just to see what gets flung over the wall of our habitual cheerfulness and isolation. Americans are fascinated when some hole opens up in the wall. It's a pause in the midst of consumerism and self-imposed isolation. It's a zoo story. It's the movement, through counterpointed characterization, toward some latent, blasted, vestigial, phantom-limb feeling for community.

There is no writer in America who liked to fling strangers more violently and gleefully toward each other than Flannery O'Connor. Whatever she may have thought of the peaceful community of the Catholic Church, she loved to see socially inept strangers pairing off, and she seems to have adored the violence that followed. Because she had no apparent interest in human love, the sensual love of one human being for another, her fictions have a feeling for the cartoonish goings-on in hell, where strangers are together because their heads are sunk into similar holes. When the inner life cannot go to God, it goes to hell, in the company of a talkative murderous misfit with no teeth. That is her sense of American communities: The psychopath who sits next to you on a Greyhound bus and who will *not* stop talking, and who has plenty of theories to fill up the time between here and Albuquerque.

In her story "A Good Man Is Hard to Find," the two essential characters seem to be the Grandmother and the Misfit. You can imagine the story existing in one form or another without several of the other characters, including Bailey or Red Sammy or June Star, but the story cannot exist without those two characters, the old woman and the psychopathic criminal. In the murderous storytelling logic O'Connor prefers, these two are meant for each other.

The Grandmother is Southern shabby genteel, rather like Blanche Dubois in this respect. She dresses properly, is a bit manipulative, and likes to cover everything up. She hides the cat, Pitty Sing, in the picnic basket, and she lies about the silver hidden in a plantation house, and her ruinous nostalgia and false witness eventually take the family near to a town appropriately named Toombsboro. There, thanks to a revelation of sorts—the old woman's recognition that she has been terribly mixed up about where she is—the accident occurs that calls forth, evokes, the Misfit and his gang.

The Misfit is a sort of Southern cracker version of the Grand Inquisitor. He is an absolute figure, signaled by the fact that he comes out of nowhere and has no Christian name. He is nearly naked when we first see him and subsequently clothes himself in the bright yellow shirt of his victim. Human laws are so much dust to him. As his gang kills off the family one by one, and that community is removed, he and the Grandmother are paired off. Gunshots ring out, and he and the Grandmother discuss eschatology, theology, and humanism. The Grandmother tries in this discussion to cling to humanism, as victims tend to do. However, the Misfit, who at least in his conversation is a fundamentalist Catholic, has both the arguments and the firepower. When the Grandmother claims to recognize the Misfit as one of her own children (a breach in the wall of isolation, a gesture toward a symbolic familial love), she reaches out to touch him, and is shot dead.

One can see in this a last, sudden conversion, a recognition, a radical swerving toward human touch, and Christian love; or a last sign of her foolishness, taking the Misfit as a member of the human community, instead of a dark angel propelled out of metaphysical darkness into the story inside a big battered hearselike automobile, near Toombsboro.

What interests me in the long final scene of this story—apart from the way the Grandmother's temporizing no longer works— is the creation of an essence between two counterpointed characters, dark and fablelike, which is externalized in a setting that suddenly and weirdly comes to life. These two characters are compatible because they both hide things and have only role names, but one believes in the ultimate force of appearances and the other does not. The image for the essence between them is the woods behind the car. The woods are monstrous. They are the product of what's given off between the Grandmother and the Misfit. They gape like an open mouth. After Bailey, the Grandmother's son, is shot, the wind moves through the woods like a "long satisfied insuck of breath." It's that word "satisfied" that signals that the entire landscape is collaborating with the Misfit and wishes to swallow the Grandmother. There's nothing around the Grandmother except those woods, that attack on her vulnerabilities. The setting itself has become hellish and surreal, with a daytime sky that is (the narrator tells us) both *cloudless and without sun.* That's the lighting in the *Inferno.* There's light, certainly, but it's sourceless. Without the Misfit, we have a mild satire on colorful Southern characters. With him, the story turns into a fiction in which one feels the breathing of a living metaphysical disorder.

There is no elegant way to move from "A Good Man Is Hard to Find" to James Joyce's "The Dead" except to observe that both stories depend absolutely on a major character coming into the story very late in its telling. In its way, "The Dead" is the greatest triangle story in English.

Because of this late introduction, the true subject of this story is rarely apparent to first-time readers until the last three or four pages. Just to list the story's characters—the Misses Morkans and their niece, Mary Jane; Freddy Malins, who drinks too much; Mr. Browne, the Protestant; Bartell D'Arcy, a tenor; Miss Ivors, the Irish nationalist—just to list these characters suggests that we will not immediately have a story of dramatic conflict so much as an evocation of a milieu, in this case the gathering of Irish friends and relatives for a social occasion on a Dublin winter night. This is important, because the milieu of Dublin, as we know from the title of the book, is a powerful one, powerful enough to endanger the freedom of its inhabitants. What can the characters do, what should these characters do, under these circumstances? This question is directed onto Gabriel Conroy early in the story. He is, in a sense, the honest center, the reader's representative: a kind, essentially decent man, who therefore resists narratability. But the story exists to challenge his decency, to challenge decency itself, and to ask what its ultimate value is.

It cannot do that, however, by counterpointing only the characters I have already named. It needs one more character I have not mentioned, a character who is missing, who has not been invited to this party; a character who appears only in the last few pages of the story, and who, by his appearance, throws all of the previous characters into a different perspective. He is the last presence to appear in the story, and he is dead—or, rather, pure spirit—by the time he arrives. But we don't know that when we enter the story, any more than Gabriel Conroy knows it. Gabriel, the nephew of the Misses Morkans, is almost as much a host as guest. Entering the story with a light fringe or shroud of snow on his shoulders, he is anxious and fretful that everything go off well, as usual. He wants to give a good after-dinner speech, and he wants the entire social occasion to succeed as it always has. He must try to control Freddy Malins's drinking, likewise the drinking of Mr. Browne. He must try to make polite conversation, and he must do this despite his real feeling that his aunts are only two ignorant old women (the story does not say that he cannot love them for this reason, only that he knows that they are ignorant).

For the first half of the story, Gabriel seems busy putting out social fires, although he ends up lighting as many as he extinguishes. Trying to be polite to Lily, he gets an outburst of bitterness about the opportunism of young men. While dancing with Miss Ivors, he is accused of not loving Ireland enough. Following her accusations, he lets loose with a line that sounds a bit like Stephen Dedalus's anger in *A Portrait of the Artist as a Young Man*: He tells Miss Ivors that he's sick of Ireland, sick of it. This quick moment of revulsion gives us a glimpse of Gabriel's weak point, a desire he has not acted on, a sickness he has done nothing for. He really wants to leave home. Instead, he has kept things as they have always been, and has lived, as it were, with his sickness concealed. He is like Johnny, the horse, later mentioned in the story, who can't do anything but go around in circles. All the same, Gabriel is the norm for most of the story: the peace bringer, a kind of social hero we are invited to admire, although this admiration is undercut later. Gabriel's outburst signals the explicit entrance of one of the story's subjects, which is the psychic cost of gentility, the keeping up of appearances despite one's actual wishes.

The party seems to go well, in any case, as does Gabriel's speech after dinner. This speech celebrates hospitality, as exemplified by Ireland and the Misses Morkans. It celebrates their beauty and charm and talent. It's a lovely, graceful, kindly, and considerate speech, something like the essence of rhetoric. It is, as we know by this time, somewhat false to Gabriel's real feelings about the party and his aunts, but it is false in the way that much socializing is false, in presenting sentiments that are pleasant to hear and without which the social world could probably not continue. This speech is, finally, an example of what social interactions tend to require.

Most of us do not have to pay immediately for our little social lies, but Joyce has arranged matters so that Gabriel has to pay for his rather quickly. His wife, Gretta, has almost disappeared in the course of the story, but we are informed that she and Gabriel have a babysitter for their children and will be spending the night in a hotel. Immediately before their leaving, Mr. D'Arcy, from upstairs, sings an air, "The Lass of Aughrim." Gabriel, standing below, sees Gretta on the landing, listening, and at first he simply does not know who she is, and then he wonders what a woman standing on the stairs in the shadow listening to music is a symbol of.

This error of wonderment leads to a tumult of errors. A few moments later, he notices the high color in his wife's cheeks and assumes that she is excited by the song and by the prospect of their coming night together. Gabriel hopes to erase "the years of their dull existence together" and to relight their souls (the metaphors are all clearly determined by this time). All the way to the hotel he is in an ecstasy of false consciousness, although we cannot be sure that it is false until we have reread the story. We assume that Gabriel is about to get his reward for being a decent man. The nature of this false consciousness is clear: He believes that his wife loves him passionately at this moment because he is sociable, charming, nice. He is wrong, but he cannot be proved wrong until the story brings in one more character, one more piece of counterpoint. The reader cannot really see the error that Gabriel has made, not yet. We don't have the other side of the contrast. We have no contrast.

Gabriel believes that it is heroic to be genteel. He believes that gentility involves sacrifices that can be rewarded with the passion that he and Gretta will share in the bed of the hotel. If we've been paying rather close attention, we might have already noticed the incompatibility of passion and gentility within the story. But it is here, in the unlit room of the hotel, where Gretta tells Gabriel about the almost allegorically named Michael Furey, a young man who once loved her and sang, "The Lass of Aughrim," and about whom she is thinking now, that Gabriel's illusions fall to pieces. In a scene of almost unimaginable delicacy, Gretta tells Gabriel that Michael Furey, her lover from years ago, stood outside her window, pitching gravel at it in the rain. Gretta was, as she says, "great with him at the time." He died for her, she says, at the age of seventeen, from a chill brought on by his reckless devotion. He caught this chill in the rain and died of pneumonia, while Gabriel, who wears galoshes, took no such risks. Michael Furey is a demon and angel lover who loved without point, who loved in order to love. The memory of him, rising to the surface at this moment, creates a condition to which Gabriel is an outsider, and his story reveals that Gretta is, indeed, not the woman he thought she was. She is not, it turns out, a symbol of anything. She is flesh and blood.

Gabriel or Michael Furey: decency or passion. The entry of Michael Furey into "The Dead" is a bit like the entry of the Misfit into "A Good Man Is Hard to Find." Passion knocks decency right off the stage. Without Michael Furey, there is no contrast. We would have a mild satire on certain Dublin types. The story would be a brilliant exercise in urban local color. But as an opposing counterpointed character, he exposes the weaknesses in

Gabriel's condition, bringing them to the surface. Gabriel immediately sees this: "He saw himself as a ludicrous figure, acting as a pennyboy for his aunts, a nervous, well-meaning sentimentalist, orating to vulgarians and idealizing his own clownish lusts, the pitiable fatuous fellow he had caught a glimpse of in the mirror." Gabriel has been the perpetrator and victim of public language, a lacquer-and-shell language of after-dinner speeches and journalism. By contrast Michael Furey has only the language of his desire, which slides toward the nonverbal: the song he sang to Gretta, and the sound of the pebbles he tossed against her window glass.

"He had a very good voice, poor Michael Furey," Gretta says.

Joyce's stories do not always have clear themes, but "The Dead" has several, one of which is, *No one will ever love you passionately for being nice.* That isn't how passionate love works. Rereading the story in the light of Michael Furey's place in it, we see that Gabriel has sentimentalized his marriage. But almost everyone does that. You get older, you put on galoshes. You can't have your after-dinner speeches and your passion too, or at least you can't buy passion with after-dinner speeches. His misunderstanding and the subsequent mood of sad tenderness in the hotel room summon the landscape of snow and sleep, just as the Misfit summons the dark insucking woods and the cloudless sunless sky. The feelings go out from the characters into the landscape, reshaping it.

From here on, everything is interfused with the presence of Michael Furey: The snow on the windowpane, tapping there, must remind him and us of Michael Furey's pebbles on Gretta's window years ago. Here, at the end of the story, Gabriel's desire for Gretta has turned into longing, and, thinking of the lonely churchyard on the hill where Michael Furey lies buried, Gabriel's soul "swooned slowly." Even the language here starts to visit Romanticism, wanting to feel it, wanting to look around, wanting to swoon.

If longing is approximately a condition of desire that cannot find its object and is therefore extended in time and space—desire stretched to its snapping point—then one might make a fair case for it as the principle emotion in *Dubliners* and its stories of people who are shut out from their own desire, prisoners for life: their glasses fogging over, shouting at their own children, standing behind iron fences as they watch the ships depart without them. Desire takes us out into a field of action, but longing leaves us perpetually shut up behind walls and locked gates, in Dublin or Winesburg or Rock Springs.

At its worst, counterpointed characterization takes us into a group mind, the last place anyone usually wants to be. A prison, a reform school, a men's club, a battalion: These groupings, in the wrong hands, can call up the human menu of types. Put two or three characters together, and you may have an essence of human relationships. Put together seven or eight, mixed by a fatigued imagination, and you get walking human clichés, rigidly controlled by the moralizing tune already created, the crushing out of character to suit the counterpoint.

The habit of human contrast, like any path of knowing, carries with it all the dangers of stereotyping and easy categorization. Gossip is usually vicious and inaccurate.

All the same, I keep thinking of music: character as melody and countermelody, the melody of the voices on the lawn, the sound of the frantic trumpet tangled around the slow and placid violins in Charles Ives's *The Unanswered Question*. "Charlie," Bernard Herrmann once asked Ives, pointing to a flute melody in Ives's *Second Symphony* that rushed above and under the strings in no pattern that he could see. "What's that flute doing?"

"Oh, that?" Ives said. "That's shadow counterpoint. That's the shadow the main theme gives off." In Ives's music, bandstand tunes and hymns and college fight songs are forced together, invited to share the same musical space in a sort of aural brawl. Ives's music likes to end with exaltation, explosions, and exhaustion.

Stories bring characters together, too, mixed and matched, sometimes pushing them toward each other like chaperones who see to it that the diffident seventh graders in dancing class are suddenly, and against all expectations, in one another's arms.

Rhyming Action

after Virgil Thomson

For the last three hundred years or so, prose writers have, from time to time, glanced over in the direction of the poets for guidance in certain matters of life and writing. Contemplating the lives of poets, however, is a sobering activity. It often seems as if the poets have extracted pity and terror from their work so that they could have a closer firsthand experience of these emotions in their own lives. A poet's life is rarely one that you would wish upon your children. It's not so much that poets are unable to meet various payrolls; it's more often the case that they've never heard of a payroll. Many of them are pleased to think that the word "salary" is yet another example of esoteric jargon.

I myself am an ex-poet. My friends the poets like me better now that I no longer write poetry. It always got in the way of our friendships, my being a poet, and writing poems. The one thing that can get a poet irritated and upset is the thought of another poet's poems. Now that I do not write poetry, I am better able to watch the spontaneous combustion of poets at a distance. The poets even invite our contemplation of their stormy lives, and perhaps this accounts for their recent production of memoirs. If you didn't read about this stuff in a book, you wouldn't believe it.

Prose writers, however, are no better. Their souls are usually heavy and managerial. Prose writers of fiction are by nature a sullen bunch. The strain of inventing one plausible event after another in a coherent narrative chain tends to show in their faces. As Nietzsche says about Christians, you can tell from their faces that they don't enjoy doing what they do. Fiction writers cluster in the unlit corners of the room, silently observing everybody, including the poets, who are usually having a fine time in the center spotlight, making a spectacle of themselves as they eat the popcorn and drink the beer and gossip about other poets. Usually it's the poets who leave the mess just as it was, the empty bottles and the stains on the carpet and the scrawled phrases they have written down on the backs of pizza delivery boxes—phrases to be used for future poems, no doubt, and it's the prose writers who in the morning usually have to clean all of this up. Poets think that a household mess is picturesque—for them it's the contemporary equivalent of a field of daffodils. The poets start the party and dance the longest, but they don't know how to plug in the audio system, and they have to wait for the prose writers to show them where the on/off switch is. In general, poets do not know where the on/off switch is, anywhere in life. They are usually *off* unless they are forcibly turned *on,* and they stay *on* until they are taken to the emergency room, where they are medicated and turned *off* again.

Prose writers, by contrast, are unreliable friends: They are always studying you to see if there's anything in your personality or appearance that they can steal for their next narrative. They notice everything about you, and sooner or later they start to editorialize on you, like a color commentator at a sports event. You have a much better chance at friendship with a poet, unless you are a poet yourself. In your bad moments, a poet is always likely to sympathize with your misery, and in your good moments to imagine you as a companion for a night on the town. Most poets don't study character enough to be able to steal it; they have enough trouble understanding what character *is*.

Of all human occupations, the writing of poetry leaves the most time for concentrated leisure activities. Poets have considerable quantities of time and a low boredom threshold, which makes them fun and scary to be around. With poets, you are likely to find yourself, as I once did, driving around town at 2 a.m. looking for a restaurant that sells roast beef sandwiches; the sandwiches, in this case, were not for the poet but for his hunting dogs, who had become accustomed to this diet. Loyalty is a religion for poets, and in any case they need the requirements of friendship to fill the other twenty-three and a half hours of the day. They are distractible, however, since they are usually thinking about an image or a favorite phrase or a new approach to the sacred. Prose writers have to spend hours and hours in chairs, facing paper, adding one brick to another brick, piling on the great heap of their endless observations, going through the addled inventory of all the items they've laboriously paid attention to, and it makes them surly—all this dawn-until-dusk sitting for the sake of substantial books that you could prop open a door with, big novels with sentences that have to go to the far right-hand margin of the page. Fiction writers get resentful, watching poets calling it quits at 9:30 a.m. Writing prose is steady work, but it tends to make prose writers grumpy and money grubbing and longfaced. They feel that they should be rewarded for what they do: observing everything and everybody with that wide-eyed staring look, like a starving cat painted on a velvet canvas.

Poets are the nobility of the writing world. Their nobility has to do with their spiritual intelligence and mind-haunted love for language and their subtle perfectionism. Poets can trace their lineage back to Orpheus, but prose writers can't go much further than that money grubber, Samuel Richardson, or that jailbird, Cervantes. Like it or not, prose fiction writers have always been part of the middle class; like other members of the middle class, they perk up when the subject turns to money. You can be a prose writer without having any kind of primary relation to the gods, but poets are often god-touched, when they are not being butchered by the gods, and this fate affects them in curious ways. They think about fate often if not obsessively. Like other nobles who spend their days scouting the heavens, however, poets have little understanding of most worldly occupations, except for writing poems and falling in love and having great sex, which is why half of their poems are about writing poems or falling in love and having great sex.

It's a good thing for prose writers that poets generally gave up telling stories in poems around the turn of the century. Each one of the English Romantic poets, with the possible exception of Shelley, was a great storyteller, and even Shelley wanted to write, with *The Cenci,* a play that could be produced on the stage; Coleridge's Ancient Mariner has a great story to tell and Keats's story of Lamia has a startlingly nightmarish quality. The story of Don Juan will keep you stimulated and alert, and even Tennyson could tell a story, although there is a softening in Tennyson that gives his narratives a gauzy mix of the medieval and the romantic that we now associate with the paintings of Maxfield Parrish. Despite their great achievements, Pound, Eliot, and Stevens and many other Modernists and Postmodernists did not care to get themselves involved with extended narratives of any kind. They saw, or thought they saw, that progressive narrative was itself a fiction and led to a progressivist view of history in which they did not believe. All their stories have turned into little shards of broken glass, each shard an enclosed historical moment, and part of the experience of reading their poems involves spending hours gluing these pieces of glass together. It is interesting to me that poets have mostly renounced telling stories in their poems, but as an ex-poet I am pleased that they have done so, because it gives me a mission in life.

The stories that poets have always liked to tell tend to be some-what hypnotic and mesmerizing. Poets have often attended to what I would call narrative echo effects. The narrative echo effect is itself an almost subvocal denial of historical progression. You see this in medieval romances and in the ballad tradition.

All ballads love repetitive actions, or cycles of doubled events. You can easily imagine stories like this. Anyone can make them up. In this summarized form, they're not particularly interest-ing, but I'll give a thumbnail example. A boy goes to a city park in the spring to fly a kite. The scene is infused with a kind of lyric innocence and bravery. The kite is yellow, and in the wind it rises so that it can hardly be seen. The narrative knows that the child is missing something, but the child does not know what this ele-ment is and could not articulate it even if he felt it directly. This is a characteristic of adolescence, having feelings without words to identify them. Conrad Aiken's stories are usually structured in this manner. Years later, when the boy has grown to be a man, he happens to walk into the same park and sees a young woman who is flying a kite. She's with another man, but her blouse is the same yellow as the boy's kite once was . . . and the man who sees her is suddenly struck with what we sometimes call déjà vu, which is only an eerie sense of some repetition, of a time spiral, of things having come around back to themselves. Now that he has words for his feelings, he's able to take some action. It's as if something about these events has started to rhyme. The effect is a bit like prophecy, except prophecy run in reverse, so that it cannot be used for purposes of worldly advancement.

Prophecy run forward gives the prophet the power of forecasting and a habit of denunciation. Prophecy run backward, into rhyming action or déjà vu, gives the participant a power of understanding. A forward prophetic power is worldly and has something to do with magic and foresight; a reverse prophecy, a sense of rhymed events, is unworldly and has something to do with insight. It moves us back into ourselves.

Robert Creeley once said about his stories, "I begin where I can, and I end when I see the whole thing returning." This is an interesting idea about certain narratives, particularly those that deal with discovery or growth. But the unsatisfactory nature of thinking about fictional form as a circle becomes apparent after a moment or two. The mechanical nature of Creeley's formulation is bothersome. Particularly in short stories, this automatic homing device would return the reader to a starting point before any initial materials in the story had been really lost from view. The immediate return of a story to its beginning would be like a rhyme that insists too quickly and bluntly on itself. Dramatically, this idea of the story as a circle would turn every journey into a trip around the block. If *every* story is a circle, ultimately returning to a source, then the sense of discovery along the way is slightly fraudulent. It has to be imaginable that any story may want to end up in a different locale from the one where it started. The return to a starting point is only a discovery if you've forgotten where you started out from in the first place. And you won't forget your starting point if you know ahead of time that you're bound to end up back there.

It's customary to talk about effective language or effective dramatic structure in fiction, but almost no one ever talks about beautiful action. At first glance, it's a dubious category. For years I have wondered about how to define beautiful action in fiction, and whether it's even possible. I don't mean actions that are beautiful because a character is doing something noble or good. I mean actions that feel aesthetically correct and just—actions or dramatic images that cause the hair on the back of our necks to stand up, as if we were reading a poem. My conclusion is that it often has to do with dramatic repetition, or echo effects. I think of this as rhyming action.

Almost every narrative struggles with two features of action in time. The first, and more common feature that I'm referring to, involves the change of a situation, its mutation into a new condition. It's what we mean when we say that in a story, something has to happen. One event follows another through a chain of causal events. The dramatic occurrences of a story push us forward toward a new state, a new condition, into the future of manifest possibilities. Any narrative that leads us toward this future also invites us to wonder or to worry how things will turn out. We turn pages, we are in suspense, we wonder whether Dr. Aziz will be convicted of doing harm to Miss Quested.

The other feature of action in narrative time, however, occurs when narratives move in reverse—when they come dramatically or imagistically to a point that is similar to one they have already seemingly passed. We see an image that we half remember. We hear a voice that we think we have heard before. We watch as someone performs an action that someone else did very much that way years ago. Something about the onward flow of time has been tricked. Poetry is interfering with the onward course of events. We *are* stepping into the same river twice. We discover that there is in fact an illusory quality about the whole concept of progression. These are the stories that poets often like to tell, but most stories have some elements of time reversal, of what I'd call stutter memories, or rhyming action. Huck Finn finds himself reliving, under Tom Sawyer's supervision, the flight and liberation of Jim, only this time in the last chapters of his book, in travesty form. In John Hawkes's *Travesty*, a trauma is being reenacted, restaged, for the second time. In Alice Munro's "Five Points" Brenda finds herself in present time accidentally playing the role of the exploited fat girl that her boyfriend Neil has told her about in a story.

Any fiction writer who begins to use the techniques of dramatic repetition can imagine the dangers it presents. A flat rhyme is more regrettable than no rhyme at all. An awkward repetition lends to any story a taste of the overdetermined and stagy. Worse, it presents all symmetries as meaningful and interesting. Not every symmetry is beautiful. The bars on a jail are symmetrical but hardly beautiful. Compulsions are often symmetrical. Neurosis often has a terrible symmetry built into it.

For this reason, I recognize that in talking about rhyming action I may be giving what amounts to bad advice to writers. Using echo effects or rhyming action can feel contrived and corny—mostly, I think, because in life we are seldom conscious of the way things come back to themselves. With that in mind, what I would argue for is the employment of rhyming action with so subtle a touch that the reader scarcely notices it. The image or action or sound has to be forgotten before it can effectively be used again. Rhymes are often most telling when they are barely heard, when they are registered but not exactly noticed.

When we see two similar events separated by time, it's as if we are watching an intriguing pattern unfolding before we know exactly what the pattern is. I don't think that the pattern has to explain itself to be beautiful. It doesn't even have to announce itself. In fact, I think it's often more effective if the echo effects, the rhyming action, are allowed to happen without the reader being quite aware of them. If the subconscious or the unconscious gets us into these time tricks, these repetitions, then it's in the subconscious or the unconscious where they should be felt.

If we lived in Poland or Bosnia, overrun for centuries by invading armies or warring factions, we might very well believe, as Polish writers have tended to believe, in the semitragic nonprogression of large historical events. Eastern European writing has a somber and sometimes lyric concern with the invisible force of the repeated act or the echoing rhyming image. Think of Kundera, of *The Unbearable Lightness of Being*, a novel that is in part a meditation on Nietzsche's concept of the eternal return, and that is filled with images concerning the impossibility of any singularity. *Once*, it turns out, is *always*, is *forever*.

African writers, with their warring factions and their history of colonialism, have produced in the twentieth century a literature much closer to Central and Eastern European literature than to ours. Bessie Head and Chinua Achebe and Wole Soyinka are, in their different ways, writers obsessed with patterns and rhyming action. Living in a new nation-state does not mean that one lives in a new state of mind. Quite the opposite.

I can imagine someone—probably an American—objecting to all this by saying that the true beauty of a story often has to do with freedom, with choice, and with the feeling of a unique action, a one-time-only occurrence happening in front of our eyes. Americans love singularity. Ah, we say, the unexpected. How beautiful the unexpected is. (No: The unexpected is seldom beautiful.) The more we talk about patterning, the more we reduce spontaneity, and the more we increase the impression of heavy-handedness, a kind of artistic overcontrol. All right, yes, perhaps. But I'm not just talking about narrative technique here anymore. I'm talking about the way some writers may view the world. Technique must follow a vision, a view of experience. No technique can ever take precedence over vision. It must be its servant. It is not the unexpected that is beautiful, but the inevitability of certain literary choices that surprise us with their sudden correctness.

In *Lolita,* the narrator, Humbert Humbert, whose name is already a double, makes a great point, in the early sections of the novel devoted to his American child-love, about her habit of chewing gum, particularly bubblegum. Much of the time when we see her, she's moving the gum around in her mouth, between words—words like "gosh"—and her half-formed sentences.

Late in the novel, long after she's been violated successively by Humbert and Clare Quilty, Humbert goes to Pavor Manor to kill Quilty, who, along with Humbert, has taken most of what it is possible to take from Lolita, including her innocence, which has been visually identified throughout the novel with her bubblegum. Humbert has violated that innocence too; they're both guilty, although Humbert is the one who feels both anger and remorse. Quilty feels nothing but contented satisfied corruption. In any case, in a scene that is horrible and comic and terrifying, Humbert finds Quilty in Pavor Manor, and after several pages of verbal confrontation, begins to shoot him. The wounding bullets seem to energize Quilty, and he trudges in a magnificent bloody progress up the stairs and down the hall until at last he arrives at his bedroom.

> "Get out, get out of here," he said coughing and spitting; and in a nightmare of wonder, I saw this blood-spattered but still buoyant person get into his bed and wrap himself up in the

chaotic bedclothes. I hit him at very close range through the blankets, and then he lay back, and a big pink bubble with juvenile connotations formed on his lips, grew to the size of a toy balloon, and vanished.

In the act of dying, Quilty visually brings forth Lolita. There she is, her visual traceries coming out of his mouth. He has taken her innocence, and it's inside him. The gum is still echoing there, but now it's grown up, gone through adolescence, and become bloody. This is a small example of a visual rhyming effect, the transformation of an image from one person to another. What better proxy than Quilty, who is both a gummy and bloody boor, to bring this image back to us?

The first sentence of the last paragraph of James Joyce's "The Dead" is a simple declarative statement: "A few light taps upon the pane made him turn to the window." It's a seemingly innocent pronouncement, and it does not force itself—or anything else—upon us. But in the previous paragraph, Gabriel Conroy has imagined Michael Furey, a "young man standing under a dripping tree," as a part of the "vast hosts of the dead" whose region he is approaching. The next paragraph begins with those few light taps upon the pane.

The narration does not say that the taps are those of falling snow until the next sentence. If we stop at the end of the sentence, and if we bother to remember what Gretta Conroy has just told Gabriel, we will remember that Michael Furey used to announce himself to Gretta by flinging pebbles and stones against her windowpane. That sound has returned. We are hearing its echo. But this time it is brought to us by the snow, which Gabriel has introduced into the story from the moment he walked into his aunts' house, scraping snow from his galoshes.

We're just far enough away from Gretta's story so that we

probably have forgotten those taps on the window. But here they are again. Although Michael Furey is dead, the same sound he created is present again at the window. All right: It's just the snow. By this time, however, the entire landscape has been transformed, so that we have entered the region of the past made manifest—the return, not of the repressed, but of the missing and the lost.

In Sylvia Townsend Warner's story "Oxenhope," published in 1971, the protagonist, a man named William, returns by car to a place in the Midlands he visited on a walking tour when he was seventeen. He had taken the walking tour at that age because he felt his mind collapsing before the pressure of adulthood and the prospect of going to a university on a scholarship. The narration describes this condition as "brain-mauling." His mind had gone empty: "All the facts he had grouped so tidily had dissolved into a broth stirred by an idiot." In his walking tour, the boy chanced upon Oxenhope and was taken in by the woman of the house, who gave him milk and scones his first night there.

The first part of Sylvia Townsend Warner's story gives us his activities and his tasks during the month that the seventeen-year-old William stayed on with his hosts at Oxenhope while his mind recovered, but it also filters these memories with William's travels now, as a retired widower of sixty-four, with a grown daughter. One of his tasks, forty-seven years ago, was to clean up the family gravestones, picking the lichen out of the inscriptions with a knife. In present narrative time, he does the job again. But what he really wants to do is return to the streams and the ponds and the lakes he remembers. His memories are narrated as self-enclosed and seemingly unrecoverable:

> The past was in the present—the narrowed valley, the steeper hills crowding into it, the river running with a childish voice....

Hauling himself up from waterfall to waterfall, here by a rowan, there by handfuls of heather, he had come to a pool, wide enough to swim a few strokes across, deep enough—though it was so clear that its pebbles seemed within hand's reach—to take him up to the neck. He had stripped and bathed in the ice-cold water, threshing about like a kelpie, and then clambered out on a slab of rock to dry in the sun. He had lain so still in his happiness that after a while an adder elongated itself from the heather roots, lowered its poised head with its delicate, tranquil features, and basked on the rock beside him. There they had lain till a hawk's shadow crossed them, and with a flick the adder was gone.

The point is made here, quietly but insistently, that happiness sometimes has a quality of invisibility to it—transparency is possibly a better word. The story is invested in the clearness of the water and the transparency of the boy. William was, in his youth, empty, harmless and unharmed, filled with bad nerves and a sense of wonder. He left no mark upon anything, he cleared and cleaned things instead, even when, as the story subsequently tells us, he went out on Cat Loch with Oliphant, the keeper of the boathouse, and caught a fish. You catch a fish and then you clean it.

Now he is an older man, having been in the foreign service, and walking around these same locales. Without putting too fine a point on it, this is not a promising situation for a short story. The baffling loss of innocence, an older man gazing at his younger self—we've certainly seen this situation before. So far, William's memories are just that: memories, and there are few situations less edifying than those in which an aging person contemplates the past. Nostalgia, after all, is usually memory raised to a level of kitsch.

Many writers would end the story right here, disastrously, with the dying fall of memory. Regret and immobility are pretty

obviously inadequate dramatic responses to the challenges of rec-
ollection and aging. The story needs something else, a counter-
movement. A good story is often like a good conversation: just
as a conversation carries with it a statement and an answer,
good dramatic structuring often involves a call-and-response.
This action—William's return to Oxenhope—calls for a return,
the action flung back on itself.

So we should not be too surprised at this point, late in the
story, when William, staring off in the middle distance of the
field, sees an almost invisible boy watching him from a hiding
place. William was once almost invisible himself. "Sliding his
glance in the direction of the watcher, he saw two brilliant pink
flowers lighting a clump of heather: two outstanding ears with the
sun shining through them. The boy had concealed himself very
well, but his ears betrayed him." Like William next to the adder,
the boy is next to the flower, but not actually concealed by it. We
don't have to remember William and the adder, however, for the
purposes of this scene, and it's not an exact rhyme anyway.

William returns to his car, the boy following him. "When
William was down and approaching his car along the grassed
road, he saw the boy approaching it from the opposite direction.
Though his ears were no longer translucent, they were certainly
the same ears." Translucency, transparency. Sylvia Townsend
Warner's story is at this point inflected with an exact intelligence
about the tactful relations between an older man and a young boy
who are strangers but are filled with a civilized interest in each
other. "The air was full of chill and poetry, and it was the moment
to put on an overcoat. Ignoring the boy, who was now standing by
the car without appearing to have stopped there, William leaned
in and released the lid of the bonnet." The boy makes a cry of surprise (the engine is at the back), and they begin to talk.

The boy takes the man to be a stranger to the area and begins to identify the valleys and the hills. Then, in a subtle shift, the boy rouses himself to tell legendary stories about the place. "'Youn's Scraggie Law,'" the boy explains. "'There was a man once, put goats on it. They were Spanish goats. They didna do.'" He then tells a story about a pool where sheep fell in and kicked each other to death. "William had heard that story from Jimmie Laidlaw," the narrator informs us. In other words, the story is at least fifty years old.

Sylvia Townsend Warner has laid down an intricate pattern here, and part of the pleasure of the story involves watching the characters work their way out of it. Observing the movement of the story, we expect the boy to give an account, a little piece of folk memory, that might have involved William when *he* was a boy in Oxenhope. This the boy does. But as it turns out, it's a visionary, apocalyptic story about Cat Loch, where William once went fishing. Here is what the boy says: "'There was a man once, set fire to it. He was in a boat, and he set fire to the water. There was flames coming up all round the boat. Like a gas ring.'" When William asks the boy what color the flames were, the boy says, "They was blue."

In the pause that follows, William remembers what actually happened forty-seven years ago. "Oliphant, interminably rowing about the loch for likely places, had thrust down his oar to check the boat's movement. Bubbles of marsh gas rose to the surface. William saw himself leaning out of the boat and touching off their tiny incandescence with a lighted match."

This is what I mean by a beautiful action. It's like a couplet. The loud apocalyptic story the boy tells, and the quiet exact memory of William setting fire to the little bubbles of marsh gas—these two go together perfectly, and they are perfectly right without anyone worrying over their symbolic applications. Apart from the precision of the language, we have been brought around in

this episode to earth, air, water, and fire and their capacity to
reintegrate someone after a brain-mauling. Furthermore, in a
last feeling for stutter memory, William is no longer transparent.
Children want to be transparent, but old people want to be permanent and visible. Through this legend, William has acquired
permanent heroic visibility. He is a song, a hero, a successful
Orpheus. Here is the story's last paragraph:

> "Jump in," William said briskly, and turned the car. When
> the surface allowed, he drove fast, to please the boy. He put
> him down at Crosscleugh (there was still a white marble dog
> in the garden) and drove on. There was no call for a backward
> glance, for an exile's farewell. He had his tenancy in legend.
> He was secure.

I have gone on about "Oxenhope" not because it's on the scale of
Lolita or "The Dead," but because in its modest way, the story creates a beautiful set of dramatic scenes that make intuitive sense.
These scenes feel right when set next to each other. And they feel
radiant before the story has been analyzed for its themes. These
images—the boy cleaning the gravestones, lying next to the adder
by a rock pool, or leaning out of the rowboat to set fire to the bubbles of marsh gas—have a quality of sensible tactile life. I don't
think the pastoral and rural setting accounts for their beauty. It's
not the countryside but the boy's wonder that transforms these
scenes, and wonder is partially created out of the rhyming action.
The boy setting fire to the bubbles of marsh gas has a place in the
story because the story has already laid before us another dramatic
scene, that of a lake of fire, which, if we bother to think about it, is
Hell, but is, otherwise, just a visionary place. Place another image
next to that one of a boy in a rowboat igniting the marsh gas with
matches, and you have, if not heaven, at least its close earthly locale.
Lazy little explosions, an afternoon of pleasing pointlessness.

"Oxenhope" doesn't force the reader into a jail of symmetrical images. It doesn't sit you up and ask if you've been paying attention. It won't, with nagging small reminders, find you inadequate as a reader. Nabokov, by contrast, with his aristocratic intelligence and fierce game playing, is capable of giving his readers a failing grade if they forget where they saw that image or that phrase before. *Pale Fire* and *Ada* can sometimes seem more like final exams than novels. They are gorgeous, in their various ways, but their symmetries gently close out much of the world. They have, at times, a suffocating overdetermined beauty.

The feeling of memory in "Oxenhope" is very light. It does not press hard on William as an adult, and its reverberations sound softly, almost inaudibly, in the reader's ear. Memory has not trapped its protagonist, because, if I understand the story properly, it has been communal. *A memory doesn't have to be accurate to be liberating,* the story claims, *it only has to be shared.*

Rhyming action exists in that curious area of writing between conscious intent and unconscious or semiconscious impulse. The writer who becomes too conscious of what s/he's doing, using this technique, would create labored and implacable symmetries. We like to think that the craft of writing is conscious and learned. That's why certain features about it can be taught. So how can I argue that the best forms of rhyming action are probably half-conscious? How can I argue for a half-conscious relaxing of the grip, for half thinking?

It feels to me as if I have worked myself into a false position. But in practice I believe it is probably not false at all. When we write, we reread what we have already written. Then, if we are not too anxious, we allow associations to mingle with those elements we have already laid down. We do so in a state of alert attentiveness that welcomes memory and progression and puts them on the same stage and then lets them go. But if we dwell on our intentions too hard, we kill the spirit. Here, in a letter, is Sylvia Townsend Warner on Benjamin Britten's opera *The Turn of the Screw*:

> The boy sang magnificently, and somehow gave the impression of singing with a hallucinated attention to what he had learned in fear and trembling and now was defiantly sure of. And it was so delicately done by the composer, with such bleak avoidance of appearing to dwell on it or turn blue that it was as matter of fact as a snake, an interval of terror and gone in a flash. Lovely!

Wonderful phrase, "bleak avoidance of appearing to dwell on it or turn blue . . ." I also love the way that quick terror, its sudden appearance and disappearance, is experienced as lovely. An event becomes beautiful without reference to its ethical character. What can be beautiful about terror? Terror is not lovely when it weighs eight hundred pounds. But when, in art, it is as light as a wingfeather, and as quick, it takes on the rapid half-lost half-found aura of the glimpse, or a dream that has lost all content but its coloration.

The act of writing anything can be as much consent as creation. One agrees to let certain passages come into the work. As a result, the story takes on a quicksilver quality, as memory drifts and glides through it.

Postscript: Sylvia Townsend Warner, for much of her adult life, intended to revise the Scott Moncrieff translation of Proust's *À la Recherche*. . . . She never got the rights from the Proust estate.

Our friends the poets are falling asleep. All this talk of memory probably annoys them. But in ceding progressive narrative to the prose writers in the twentieth century, they have also, in large part, given over the poetry of memory. The poetry of memory in this century belongs to Proust and Faulkner and Woolf and Achebe and the others. It is more difficult to say that the Modernist poets wrote the poetry of memory. *The Cantos* is an act of cultural memory but not in equal part personal memory. True also of *The Waste Land*. American poets, in this alarming century, have more often insisted on memory-as-trauma. When one thinks of the poetry of memory in this century, one thinks of the shocks that those memories have sustained. An insistence on memory-as-trauma, however, demonizes the entire realm of remembrance—it demonizes, I would say, one's entire foundation of experience in the past. This demonization is one that many poets have bravely explored. But trauma is not a progressive narrative. It is a loop. It begins where it can, and ends when it sees the whole thing returning.

But when it is not traumatized, the action of memory on our present life may be closest to the feeling that rhyme creates, not full rhyme, but half rhyme, assonance, slant rhyme. One of the features I love about Wordsworth's *The Prelude* is that, although it is written in blank verse, the events within the poem contain a rhyming logic. Memory does not have to attach itself to its replica in our present moments. It can be oblique, sidling, scary and luminous in its distant relatedness to us. The tree branch, the one without bark outside my window now, does not remind me of another tree branch, nor even a bare arm. That would be too easy. It reminds me of something else. And those broken strings hanging from the basketball hoop are like nothing so much as dangling spider webs I remember from . . . another time. What are these trace memories, these images, but visitors or visitations from our pasts? The best visitors are the shy ones. They hardly want to come in. They stand at the doorway. If you look at them too closely, they'll probably run away and disappear.

We have to save them. We have to save them by turning away a little, pretending to do something else, like lifting the hood of the car and tinkering with the engine, before they'll befriend us. These memories, our children, are not all demons. To claim that *all* memory is demonized and traumatic is to count oneself among the permanently damned.

Paradise is less plausible than Hell, but it is surely no less real.

Note

Virgil Thomson, "Survivors of an Earlier Civilization," in *The State of Music* (New York: Vintage, 1962): 37–53.

Maps and Legends of Hell:
Notes on Melodrama

Certain subjects, like melodrama, have a tendency to transport a person back to the aromatic scenes of childhood. In my case, it's the Tonka Theater, stinking of rancid buttered popcorn, in Excelsior, Minnesota, where the first aesthetic response of my life was enacted, at age five. I crawled under the seat to escape from the images passing on the screen. The movie that did this to me was *Snow White and the Seven Dwarfs*. I don't remember the actual crawling, although it was reported to me, and I don't remember much of the movie except for the wart on the witch's nose, and the redness of her cartoon apple. I am not certain if my memory is correct on this point, but I think a single hair was growing out of that wart. My friends the cineastes tell me I am misremembering that movie. I don't care; it doesn't matter now. I saw *something*: I remember the witch's psychotic condition as she sat in front of her mirror thinking that she could get into a beauty contest with Snow White. Before she turned herself into an old crone, with the nose and the wart, she was sleek and corrupt, like a female Ming the Merciless. What craziness was that? It wasn't just that she was corrupt, although her looks could stop a truck. She was insane.

I didn't, of course, have words like "insane" or "psychosis" in my vocabulary. If I had, I might not have hidden under the seat.

Melodrama, like villainy, is one of those literary and conceptual categories that repels serious thought. In the minds of most readers, melodrama is a recognizable failure of reason and feeling, even a failure of imagination itself. And yet it is almost endlessly interesting to puzzle over. It's *engaging*. The subject leads through a series of tangles and confusions back toward sex and power and religion and the presence or absence of religious ideas. Melodrama is also puzzling because of the grip it sometimes applies, like sensationalism or pornography, to the imagination. Liking it makes people feel guilty. Because melodrama is about, among other things, the failure of explanations, it calls forth the imagination in compensation. For this reason, the lyric arts don't have to worry about melodrama in the same way that the narrative arts do. People don't talk about melodramatic poetry very much, even though it certainly exists. Probably the word itself is one of those conceptual grab bags: No one can agree what is inside it.

All the same, general and polite agreement exists among intelligent readers that melodrama—whatever it is—is deplorable. Children might enjoy it, but a healthy adult mind should be able to resist it. Workshop writers claim to disdain it. Reviewers point at it with somewhat stagy alarm. A friend of mine once described melodramatic writing as containing "emotional violence" against the reader, and she wasn't wrong. One often feels bullied in its presence, pushed around. It's generally understood to involve a failure of intelligence or understanding, or both. In its sphere of influence, aesthetic violence substitutes for proper dramatic action and evidence.

Melodrama has turned from being a descriptive category into being a category of complaint, a category that also contains complaint, and what's interesting about this transformation is that as the word becomes more of a tool of accusation, its meaning becomes vaguer. In this respect its history has some similarities to the history of the words "romantic" and "romanticism." The definition of "melodrama" has become a small but important event in the history of taste. Critics like Peter Brooks who have taken some care to define melodrama as a purely literary form (in *The Melodramatic Imagination*) have performed a wonderful service. All the same, the word's common meaning continues to slip away from a precise academic definition and instead is used for the purposes of blame and abuse.

People who are quarreling will often, after a particularly wounding accusation, accuse the other of being melodramatic. "Oh, don't be so melodramatic!" they will cry.

We need the word to point to something in human life for which there is no other term. The trouble is that this "something" is extremely hard to get at, because, I think, it's a quality or essence we generally don't like or would prefer not to acknowledge. As a form it grows out of straightforward blindness: the witch gazing into her mirror and not recognizing that she looks like a CEO and not a beauty queen. It's important that the witch is powerful, that she has magic; it may be that her psychosis has something to do with her magic. Also, she hates. She hates Snow White not because of what Snow White has done but because of what she *is*—beautiful. The witch is powerful and insane and unfair and ugly. Narratively, she's much more interesting than Snow White. We just don't want to *be* with her.

It's a hopeless exercise, at least for me, to define melodrama as a purely literary category. Instead, I want to use the term to get at some features of writing and thinking associated with the invisibilities of power. For reasons that I hope to make clear, I think the word "melodrama" will go on, however unfairly, being used to categorize certain kinds of aesthetic misjudgments and mistakes. A word gets misused because there aren't other words for what we mean, a common form of verbal degradation.

An instance: I once had a rumpled and messy friend who was a colleague where I worked. The crucial word here is "once." Most offices have someone around like this person. He was, for a time, unfailingly helpful to young faculty members. He invited them for dinner. A great raconteur and gourmet, he could cook and talk simultaneously and brilliantly. He loved to help out people who were in a weak position. In this role, he was lovable. When they established themselves, when they no longer depended on him, he dropped them. He invented imaginary crimes that they had committed and wouldn't speak to them and would pass them in the hallways without nodding. He insisted on betrayal. He went away for a year and when he came back he was speaking to almost no one. *Everyone* had betrayed him, it seemed.

Because there was no easy accounting for his behavior, his ex-friends couldn't stop talking about him. They would apologize sheepishly for what they were going to do and then launch into some new inadequate theory. After a while, my colleagues simply said he was evil—on a very modest scale, of course, compared to the villains of our climate. But this strategy permitted them to close the subject and move on to another field of office politics.

Many of the elements of melodrama kick into this account—the dichotomy of the powerful and powerless, inexplicable betrayal, moral polarization, elements of the Pygmalion story festering inside it, and the resort to a religious category to put the whole matter to rest—but what interests me most about my ex-friend was that everyone thought that his behavior was unforgivable. If an explanation existed for his behavior, no one could find it. For that reason, he became notorious, story-worthy, more interesting than the rest of us, and memorable.

Compare that instance with another: Three or four years ago, before Jimmy Swaggart was publicly accused of various moral failings, he commanded a good deal of television time. My son, who was then about nine years old, was mesmerized by these performances, although he did his best to laugh them off. I would find him in the kitchen eating a sandwich and watching Jimmy Swaggart. I thought he was afraid of Swaggart, and it wasn't hard to see why: the bullying, the accusations, the waving of the sacred word in the air, the recourse to unanswerable authority, the threat of terrible endless punishment originating from an unseen and possibly implacable source. It was strong medicine for a secular household.

One morning I switched on one of Swaggart's programs but, as an experiment, kept the sound off. Here's what I saw: a physically powerful sweating man, shouting, red-faced, furiously angry, pointing his finger, pacing back and forth, unstoppable. I knew he was making accusations and demanding abnegation. People came forward and asked him for forgiveness.

I don't mean to explain Swaggart away by saying what I'm about to say, nor do I claim any originality for the following observation. All the same, what I saw on the television set with the sound turned down was a man who looked like a drunken father who had just come home on Saturday night and had gotten everybody up and was promising them the worst beating they had ever had. Swaggart looked like a drunk. Not just a drunk but a mean drunk, who was also, dangerously, a family man. He paced and shouted and pointed. His audience—his congregation—looked as if they recognized him.

Or maybe they didn't exactly recognize him, and that was why he had power over them. To be inside the power of the performance is to be in a state where you want to crawl under the seat or act quickly to stop what may happen from happening. I don't think this is quite the same as suspense, although suspense is implicated in it. It has more to do with the infliction of pain from an unknown source, that is, a source that doesn't have to answer for itself. And the whole drama has to do with the dynamics of power and the mechanisms by which power does or does not forgive, does not inflict the pain it is capable of inflicting.

A common cliché among writing workshops is that good writing must be fair to all the characters and give adequate explanations for all forms of behavior, however bad they may be. Chekhov is usually cited here as the supremely unmelodramatic and comprehensively truthful and fair tale-teller. I will have more to say about that in a minute. I have heard, from one famous teacher of writing, that the writer should take the "God viewpoint." This viewpoint, being that of God, understands everything, and, like God, forgives everything equally.

This position is not the God viewpoint at all. It's the Enlightenment viewpoint, which is hardly the same thing. The history of Christianity is nagged by the story of God's refusal to understand and forgive everybody. It is nagged by God's righteousness, and the dramatic locale for that refusal, its proof, is Hell. In order for Hell to be hell, two conditions at least must be in operation: God must refuse to understand certain conditions and to forgive certain actions whether their causes are understood or not; and the perpetrators of these actions must not, or cannot, ask for forgiveness properly. This, and their actions while alive, constitute their villainy. The eternal fire and the suffering are *almost* secondary. They're not actually secondary because the mechanisms that are at work bring forth the infliction of pain.

Hell is a threatening puzzle for Christians. How it was created in a cosmos governed by a loving and just God, and why it is perpetuated—in effect, why evil continues to exist if God is all-powerful—constitutes one of Christianity's central mysteries and articles of faith. Dante's vision of Hell is, of course, much more interesting to most readers than his vision of Paradise. To put it another way, perhaps most readers never get to paradise. Hell, being both place and condition, brings forth the refusal of God to stop punishing. Besides, punishment is more narratively picturesque than pleasure. At the same time, Hell's very existence presupposes that God is not willing to comprehend all actions equally. Some things God *doesn't* forgive. Viewed from a distance, Hell is the proof of God's failure or refusal to love. For that reason, among others, Hell is more confounding and dramatically, if not poetically, memorable than Paradise, where almost nothing happens.

Say what you will about it, Hell is story-friendly. If you want a compelling story, put your protagonist among the damned. The mechanisms of Hell are nicely attuned to the mechanisms of narrative. Not so the pleasures of Paradise. Paradise is not a story. It's about what happens when the stories are over. Furthermore, Paradise often feels implausible in a way that Hell never does.

Melodrama, typically, is the scene of the incomprehensible attached to the unforgivable. It is powered by the force of the demonic, particularly in its capacity and willingness to hurt. The inability of Western narrative art to get rid of melodrama has something to do with the clear evidence on the world scene in contemporary history that large numbers of people are willing to massacre, to kill and hurt, without remorse—those with power to hurt *will* do it, blindly, smilingly, unthinkingly. They have done it in Bosnia, in Cambodia, and in our cities; they did it in Germany and Argentina and the Soviet Union. We have histories now of mass tortures, mass murders.

Andrew Delbanco has argued cogently that we have lost, as a living imaginative entity, the evil angel whose behavior is dramatically compelling but virtually inexplicable. Every one of Satan's actions must be perfectly evil, nothing less, just as every one of God's actions must be perfectly good. Satan as a figure is dead, but evil continues, without, however, someone to answer for it. Evil is more evil than ever, even when we have no name for it and no Satanic figure to blame for it. We still have melodrama, however: the honorable narrative house of horror and the unforgivable.

For Nietzsche, Christianity was a catastrophe for the imagination. Obsessed and tormented by its dualisms, Nietzsche imagined into verbal life an art, if not exactly a moral system, that would move "beyond good and evil," an art that would capture what he considered the joy and energy of classic Greek tragedy and poetry. But because Nietzsche never gives up power as an originating category, the quietism that he seems from time to time to be advocating never arrives fully described on the field of his philosophy. Instead, Nietzsche's distaste for the romance of powerlessness, which he equates with the lowest form of thought—Christian piety—brings back in disguised form the redemption that had been seemingly banished, redemption in the form of the Overman, whose presence in Nietzsche's writing is more felt than seen.

Nietzsche's efforts to turn everything upside down nevertheless preserve demonism in a new form, although this time ascribed to Christianity, and sainthood, which is as difficult to achieve under Nietzsche as it was under Christ. Nietzsche never did pass beyond dualistic and psychologically reductive reasoning. The pleasure in reading him derives from watching thought trying to get beyond good and evil by virtue of its own brilliance. His philosophy is very much in the struggle-and-triumph mode; one might say that Nietzsche's philosophy is not only about melodrama, it *is* melodrama.

Scholars like Peter Brooks place melodrama within a clear historic period, particularly from the 1860s onward. The features he describes can be retrofitted to Elizabethan tragedy, at the very least. The moral polarization, the expressive gestures that must substitute for what cannot be said, the mysterious and inexplicable logic at the heart of wrongdoing, the scrutiny, as Brooks calls it, of "a blank at the center of existence that evidently contains the key to existence if one only knew how to read its message"—all these are apparent in drama and tragedy that precedes the actual coining of the word "melodrama," which, strictly speaking, has to do with the stage presentation of music and expressive gesture. Because so much of melodrama as we now understand it involves innocence being hurt and deprived of power by the unknowably malign, it is drawn toward stories about women, children, and minorities deprived unjustly of their rights, as the critic Martha Vicinus has shown. It has functioned and can function politically for exactly that reason.

Melodrama is the recognition, dramatically, that understanding sometimes fails, articulation fails, and enlightenment fails. It is transfixed by injustice but can call for improvement. Fascinated by what is unforgivable, melodrama dramatizes villainy. Cataclysmic moral conditions erupt in it. It seems to stand on the side of enlightenment in its exposure of the corruption of the powerful and in its sympathy for the downtrodden; but it seems to stand on the side of conservatism in its assertion of constant struggle and in its belief in the perpetual existence of evil and the unknowability of its ultimate source.

Melodrama at its worst exaggerates a certain neurotic feature of fiction, that is, the habitual creation of conflict and polarities. Even Freud placed, as Peter Brooks observes, *das Unbewusste,* the unconscious and unknown, at the center of precipitating action and neurotic distortion. At their best, melodramatic elements give energy and power to the work of writers as disparate as Dostoyevsky, Henry James, Thomas Hardy, Edith Wharton, Richard Wright, Vladimir Nabokov, Katherine Anne Porter, Emily Brontë, Toni Morrison, Thomas Pynchon, Ernest Hemingway, Raymond Carver—to name only a few writers from the modern period.

The problem with melodrama is not mindlessness. Mindlessness is ascribed to it by people who think that melodrama must be equated with a hero and villain locked in a death-struggle on an ice floe headed toward Niagara Falls, or Our Hero struggling in an abandoned steel mill with a sweaty muscle-bound death-crazed biker Nazi. Melodrama's problem, really, is its family relation to kitsch. Its defining origin in French popular theater has stuck with it in mass entertainment. Everywhere it is associated with vulgarity. The word "melodrama" is now used almost universally as a pejorative term, and it is understood to be a series of writerly moves, even ways of feeling or thinking, that should be avoided. As a result, many young writers, and perhaps experienced ones as well, may be reluctant to have conflicts or plots *in any form* in their stories because they fear that such elements will be branded as melodramatic, vulgar, and cheap. These people, standing up for art, will nevertheless read Thomas Hardy and Edith Wharton with approval and in guilty pleasure go off to movies with heroes and villains and stylized conflicts.

Because melodrama lends itself to schlock and kitsch, the form as a whole has been contaminated, particularly in the eyes of those who would rather not engage the world of action at all, or who may feel that sensibility and style can function redemptively. To be fair, any story that wishes to be free of the categories of good and evil, or that wishes to decenter fixed moral coding, will certainly operate outside the orbit of melodrama. Many of the stories that depend on understandable conflict or what Grace Paley in one of her stories calls "the open destiny of life" will find themselves in a different literary universe. Countless different modes of telling stories do not call upon it in any way. But that doesn't mean that melodrama is dishonorable, or that its presuppositions are stupid. As a form, it conveys to any story a quality of urgency—a sense that the stakes are very high. This aura of urgency is typically what directs one's attention to it. Melodrama not only compels attention but sustains it. Melodramatic elements don't guarantee schlock, any more than the sonnet form guarantees quality or high-mindedness.

In melodrama, those with the power to hurt *are* enacting that power. In such situations, melodrama informs us, words fail. Melodrama commemorates this feeling for mute disaster. That's one reason why minorities forced into silence love it. Billy Budd stutters and spits as he tries to answer Claggart. Mr. Helton, in Katherine Anne Porter's "Noon Wine," can't say much of anything to defend himself, and, late in the story, neither can his employer. Othello has nothing like Iago's smoothly subtle articulations. Edith Wharton's Lily Bart can never say the right words to her subtle accusers. In some sense, she can't even *find* them. Pynchon's Oedipa Maas has been struck dumb by her experiences, and *The Crying of Lot 49* ends with her silence.

Sometimes, the more you hear, the less you understand what you're hearing. The more you see, the less you recognize. The face of maliciousness is greatly detailed but in some fundamental sense unreadable. You can't reply because you can't meet its gaze. This is its relation to hysteria, the blaze of emotions caught inside disarticulation.

Quoting Victor Serge, Wallace Stevens in "Esthétique du Mal" speaks of the queasiness one feels when confronting the articulate malign: "I followed his argument / With the blank uneasiness which one might feel / In the presence of a logical lunatic." The logical lunatic here is Lenin. Earlier in the poem, Stevens announces, "The death of Satan was a tragedy / For the imagination. A capital / Negation destroyed him in his tene-ment / And, with him, many blue phenomena." This is Stevens *contra* Nietzsche. Logical lunacy in the poem takes the place or rather fills the slot vacated by Satan. For Stevens, the smooth talker becomes the logical lunatic.

The death of Satan is hardly the death of opposition or antagonism, but what one notices, following Stevens's com-ment about the "tragedy for the imagination," is the death in much modern American fiction not only of Satan but also of the antagonist—*any* antagonist. It's as if everybody has finally agreed about everything except what kind of sensibility to have. The avoidance of conflict in such fiction has to do with a pho-bia toward melodrama and its popular degradations, but it also involves a refusal to engage the world altogether. This refusal is a luxury of writers in a rich hegemonic culture. The death of the antagonist implies a refusal on the part of protagonists and their authors to make any kind of move in any direction. Such a refusal spells the apparent death of desire and an elevation of "voice" or "style"—the hallmarks of privatized individualism—but actually involves its concealment. When apparent desires melt away, antagonists do, too.

The trouble is that desires never quite leave the stage in this manner. They go underground, where Eros *will* have its day. We are perhaps unfortunately in the age of underground or priva-tized experience. Instead of the front porch, we have the back deck, concealed of course by high redwood fences that permit us to indulge ourselves in new ways. Stories in which desires are quieted, and from which the antagonist has disappeared, are grounded, if that is the word, in drift and privacy and a sort of aesthetic sadism. Stories in which desire meets resistance in private are often about hysteria, which is melodrama that has come in through the back door and which exists almost entirely at the psychological level. Ernest Hemingway's stories are usually locked in situations of this kind, and men—wounded in the ways that Hemingway often insists upon—are the ones in the grip of his fiction's resulting hysteria.

To argue against melodrama, you would have to be a creature of the Enlightenment or of irony, or both, and you would have to believe that all actions are understandable, explainable, and forgivable. Reform is possible, infinitely. Human beings are perhaps not perfectible, but we should act as if they are. Given the right social order, self-possession and self-containment will be the order of the day. We can glimpse this world-feeling in some of Mozart's operas (though not *Don Giovanni*), certain of Tolstoy's stories, and the novels of Jane Austen, among other manifestations. In Whitman's poetry there is a deep faith in both the power of statement and understanding, prior to the enacted song of cosmic forgiveness.

Like the poor, however, melodrama will in all likelihood always be with us. Here it is, announcing itself mindfully in Robert Stone's *Dog Soldiers.* Converse is sitting on a bench in Saigon with a lady who is a missionary in Ngoc Linh. He asks her what kind of a religion they have in Ngoc Lihn, and she replies that it isn't a religion; they worship Satan. Converse says that he himself doesn't believe in Satan.

"It's always surprised me," she said softly, "things being what they are and all, that people find it so difficult to believe in Satan."

"I suppose," Converse said, "that people would rather not. I mean, it's so awful. It's too spooky for people."

"People are in for an unpleasant surprise." She said it without spite as though she were really sorry.

Whatever else this passage may do, it surely and certainly announces to the reader that the novel s/he has started will contain a plot, several antagonists, and the presence of slightly incomprehensible wrongdoing. Something wicked this way comes. *Dog Soldiers* has all these features—Converse never quite understands why even he acts in the way he does—but the presence of such features does not seem all that surprising in a novel about the smuggling and selling of heroin from Vietnam to the United States. The missionary lady sitting on the park bench is obviously a piece of string to connect emotional and thematic points of the story. Many readers would be more surprised to find exactly these features in Anton Chekhov's stories, where they exist less visibly.

In Chekhov, melodrama is disguised under an apparent narrative equanimity. Chekhov as a writer is seemingly antimelodramatic at every turn. The voice remains calm, and one feels—I should say that *I* feel—in the hands of a storyteller who is lovably and blissfully sane, full of sense and good humor. When, in "The Bishop," the title character is addressed by his first name, at last, on his deathbed, the readjustment of his and the story's perspective is somehow clarifying and beautiful. We are able to see that the adjectives that have been attached to us will ultimately slip away. We will become nouns and verbs. Nobody cares about the titles, anyway. Or the adjectives either. It's not that we're all children in Chekhov's fiction; we're just more transparent.

But in his story "In the Ravine," which Tolstoy considered Chekhov's masterpiece, we can see the mechanisms of intelligent melodrama deployed with great subtlety. They are there to claim a stake that is both personal and social. "In the Ravine" is a descent into a kind of hell. Hell, however, in Chekhov's version is largely comprehensible. Largely, I think, but not entirely.

The narrative takes its time in descending to its smelly locale, the town of Ukleyevo, a place where prosperity, such as it is, depends on a textile plant. With his usual interest in specific facts, Chekhov tells us that the community stinks of the acetic acid used in the processing of cotton. The narrative explains in considerable and convincing detail why the factory waste is necessary to the economic life of the town, and it introduces us to Stepan and Anisim, two brothers who stand to inherit their father's grocery and some of his wealth if he approves of their wives.

Stepan marries Aksinya. She is beautiful, a hard worker, ambitious and aggressive, and she compensates for her husband's deafness and vagueness with pure human force. "She was always laughing and shouting," the narrator says. The other brother, Anisim, having not taken matters into his own hands, is married off to a peasant woman, Lipa, "a thin, pale-faced fragile girl with fine, delicate features and her skin was tanned from working in the open air."

The long wedding-and-reception scene at the center of the story has a feeling of tender social satire, very similar in its mood to the way the friends and family groupings are presented in Joyce's "The Dead." Everyone at first seems pleasant enough. But on second glance they're not. Small details start to appear like poisonous mushrooms in the shady spots where the sun never reaches. Speaking of the town council, Chekhov's narrator observes:

They had lived on lies for so long, it seemed that even the skin
on their faces had taken on a peculiarly criminal complexion all of its own. The clerk's wife, a scraggy woman with a
squint, had brought all of her children along; just like a bird
of prey she looked at the plates out of the corner of her eye and
grabbed everything within reach. . . .

At this moment we arrive at a crucial juncture in the story, a
point of no turning back. Chekhov's narration is about to make
a commitment. This is a critical moment in any melodrama.
The "criminal complexion" and the bird of prey imagery pre-
pare us for the moral costume in which Aksinya is about to be
dressed. An attitude is about to be transposed into an essence.
Chekhov is leading up to the claim that Aksinya is a particular
kind of person. She has one kind of character and no other. It
doesn't matter how hard she works or how much she laughs
and shouts.

Here she is, then, in Ronald Wilks's translation, looking upon
the wedding guests:

Aksinya had gray, naïve-looking eyes that seldom blinked and
a naïve smile constantly played over her face. There was something snake-like in those unblinking eyes, in that small head
and long neck, in that shapely figure. As she surveyed the
guests in her green dress with its yellow front, she resembled
a viper peering up out of the young spring rye at someone
walking past—its body erect and head raised high.

That snake image is the marker of a writerly verdict. Aksinya
is a snake, and thus constitutes a destiny for the rest of the story.
No matter what else may be said about Aksinya, the tone of most
subsequent actions has been established. Most melodramas have
a moment like this one. Decisions have been made about the
characters, and the unfolding of the story can only be under-

stood in light of those decisions. There's no going back from it. You can argue that writers shouldn't judge their characters so conclusively, but you would have to claim in the same breath that people are always alterable, that no one is incorrigible. You would have to argue that the word "incorrigible," applied to humans, is meaningless. It's possible to make that argument, but difficult, and, in our time, unusual.

Aksinya's snakiness puts the reader directly into one of the primal myths of our culture. She's *placed*. Now, two pages later, here is Lipa:

> The moment her husband left, Lipa changed completely and became bright and cheerful. In her bare feet, with her sleeves tucked right up to her shoulders, she washed the staircase in the hall and sang in a thin, silvery voice. And when she carried the huge tub full of dirty water outside and looked at the sun with that childish smile of hers, she was like a skylark herself.

Moral polarities; expressive gestures; a certain obscure opposing devilishness. Chekhov is fair to Aksinya (life is a struggle in Ukleyevo, people have to be tough) but fair only up to a point. That point is the moment when most people reach the equivalent of a moral conclusion and decide to stick to it.

"However much evil existed in the world," the narration says, "the night was still calm and beautiful." Calm and beautiful, that is, to Lipa. She has the feeling that "someone was looking down on them from the very heights of heaven." The tone of the story does not change much as these two polarities are established. It stays calm, the kind of calm van Gogh describes in one of his letters: "calm amidst the catastrophe." Lipa gives birth to a baby boy, Nikifor. Aksinya grows more jealous and envious and greedy. One day, as Lipa is doing the laundry Aksinya arrives, shouts accusations, and then in a kind of fugue state pours boiling water from a ladle over the baby.

> A scream rang out, the like of which had never been heard in Ukleyevo and it was hard to believe it came from such a frail little creature as Lipa. Suddenly all was quiet outside. Without so much as a word, Aksinya went back into the house, with that same naïve smile on her face . . .

Following Nikifor's death, Chekhov's story shows very little interest in reproducing the actual dynamics of grief. Those feelings belong to Lipa but not to the reader or to the story. In a narrative move characteristic of Chekhov, we see Lipa trying to tell an old man about her loss, but eloquence escapes her. The old man understands her anyway, but his understanding brings her no comfort. "Well, you're a mother," the old man says. "Every mother feels sorry for her child." Comfort may exist in the story, but it is unavailable to most of the characters. Lipa leaves the village with her mother, distracted and miserable but surrounded by the story's detached sweetness. Aksinya is not brought to justice. Ukleyevo goes on in its usual way. Power, as Chekhov knew very well, destroys innocence and frailty; the moral issues are perfectly obvious, but the drama makes them felt.

"In the Ravine" is a melodrama that is narrated with such equanimity that the melodramatic elements are all but camouflaged—camouflaged but not invisible. Behind the baby's death is Aksinya's greediness and emotional dissociation, and behind her greediness is Ukleyevo's tentative communal interest in the accumulation of capital, but no explanation is sufficient. How does anyone explain the act of pouring boiling water on a baby? Explanations stop at a certain point. It's this point that Chekhov seems so interested in, when facts lead us toward metaphor, and people start to appear as snakes and skylarks.

Withholding judgment no longer seems possible or particularly desirable. It just starts to seem beyond any human capacity.

The guilty pleasure of melodrama: saying that someone is bad or good, and believing it; giving into a feeling for essences. In my case, giving in meant reading Davis Grubb's *The Night of the Hunter* in high school and suspecting that the mad preacher Harry Powell chasing the boy, John, and his sister, Pearl, all over hell's half-acre had something to do with my life. I loved the nightmarishness of the book, its austere lyricism, its feeling for inane malevolence.

For the sake of tolerance and pluralism, it's important sometimes to make good faith efforts to resist those feelings. The soul-stirrings of revolution often do. Revolution points toward perfectibility and the kinds of people who are standing in the way. The capacity of storytelling in both fiction and poetry to open possibilities, to enlarge the field of understanding, is the angel-side of rationality. It holds out the possibility of a better world, the joyfulness of cooperative anarchy. No healthy person would want to live in a nightmare. Furthermore, not all nightmares need to be true. Their monstrous metaphors may feel alive but need not stalk us during our waking hours.

Against the metaphysics of melodrama, we can recognize the capacity of people to speak to each other, to converse, to live together, to change. To make, as Grace Paley's wonderful phrase has it, "enormous changes at the last minute." Her book of that title is one of the few contemporary classics of the American short story. It's also one of the few stylish classics of American progressivist, even anarchist, fiction. I love the book's openheartedness, its combative pacifism, its voices and feeling for urban life, for gritty lives and pugnaciousness. The book holds a range of characters, but for the most part these characters aren't slotted into moral pigeonholes. Paley's characters have hopes, but these hopes are intelligent and sly and sharp-witted. They do what they do in a Nietzschean way—no deep subjectivities here, no extended gloomy introspections, and no sickening need for redemption, either—and when they do something wrong, they have their reasons. If their reasons are bad, the fault is usually with the political/economic set-up, but there's no insistence anywhere on essences—the stories love most forms of singularity—and, the book seems to insist, enormous changes are always possible. No plot is so fixed that it cannot be altered. There is no nightmare we cannot wake up from.

I want to speak against this understanding of *Enormous Changes at the Last Minute*. I want to make an effort to enlarge the book. I do not think that the version I have just given of the stories is wrong, exactly, but it is certainly incomplete. My feeling about the stories is that they are often darker than they are given credit for. They want to talk *about* the darkness, or *to* the darkness, but when this intention becomes apparent, so does melodrama. The stories have an occasional but intense interest in exactly the elements that give rise to melodrama, and as often as the sensibility seems to be escaping from melodrama, it yields to it. Because Grace Paley's sensibility as an anarcho-progressivist is so well known, the appearance of melodrama in her stories is a bit unsettling.

To return to the image with which I began this essay: Melodrama occasionally grows out of a situation in which someone looks but doesn't see what is there. It doesn't *register*. Romantic poetry contains several moments of this sort: Christabel gazing at Geraldine, Cortez's soldiers staring at him as he stares at the Pacific. Wild surmise takes the place of comprehension. The object is in front of you but you've never seen its like. The Romantics want to make this moment one of joyous wonderment, a moment of symbolic rebirth, but it has a way of turning horrific, particularly in Coleridge and Keats. One wakes up in an unknown region, a cold hillside, having advanced over unusual thresholds. A feeling for this moment arrives in Robert Stone's recent novel *Outerbridge Reach,* as the protagonist views the sun through a window on a remote Pacific island:

> Each warped ball was the reflection of another in an index glass, each one hung suspended, half-submerged in a frozen sea. They extended forever, to infinity, in a universe of infinite singularities. In the ocean they suggested there could be no measure and no reason. There could be neither direction nor horizon. It was an ocean without a morning, without sanity or light.

"A universe of infinite singularities" is one of utter madness. It's a distance from this madness to Grace Paley's stories, but the distance is not so large as to defy comprehension. In "Conversation with My Father" the narrator is quarreling amiably with her ailing father about storytelling. The father is sick and in bed; his daughter brings in possible stories to keep him involved in the matters of life. He is, as we would say, old-fashioned. He wants to know the background of characters, what their parents were like, what people they came from. He acknowledges chains of cause and effect in a way that his daughter, the writer, would rather not. She dislikes plot, "the absolute line between two points which I've always despised." An optimist and a progressive, she believes, she says, that "everyone, real or invented, deserves the open destiny of life."

She tells him a story about a woman who lives with her son across the street. The son becomes a junkie, "which is not unusual in our neighborhood." The woman becomes a junkie too in order to be close to her child. But the son, "in disgust," gives up his habit and leaves the city and his mother.

This is the inner story. In the outer story, the storyteller and her father argue. The father wants to know more about the people. He wants details. The storyteller wants to counter this wish for details with a story that does justice to the characters: "You can't even think of an ending good enough."

So the daughter tells her father a revised story with more details. In this revised story the son and his girlfriend give up their habit, but the mother still keeps it. Habit is a begetter of plot. Compulsion and addiction and secrecy are its children. After hearing the new version, the father agrees that the ending is correct, that the woman in the story is "sick" (so is he) and that it is a "tragedy." Hearing these words, his daughter is horrified. She starts to beg—that is the verb used—for him to see it some other way. In an aside, she admits that her new happy ending, cooked up for her father, is not like life, "which unlike me has no pity." She tells him that the woman recovers, gets better, becomes a credit to her community.

"No," her father says, "truth first." He tells her that as a writer "that's your main trouble. You don't want to recognize it. . . . In your own life, too, you have to look it in the face." He feels worse and takes a couple of nitroglycerin tablets. His daughter claims that the woman reforms. The father denies it. And he has the last word in the story. "Tragedy! You too. When will you look it in the face?"

Of course what she is looking at in this narrative moment is her own father's face. He is a dying man. For him, there is no "open destiny" of any kind. Political and social good intentions are running up here against the old man's realism and bad health. And what this realism and bad health are accusing the narrator of is selective well-meaning blindness. He asserts (against her) that she looks into the mirror and doesn't acknowledge what she sees. Her resistance to plot, her resistance to information about family background of the sort given by writers he likes such as Turgenev and Chekhov, is also a resistance to death. It's understandable and heroic, but it's wishful because it denies necessity, and the old man recognizes her wishfulness more clearly than she does.

The stories in this book are wry and energetic and good-humored, but they are dampened by a melancholy that seeps in at odd moments. The content of that melancholy is the recognition that there are some singular matters most well-intentioned people can't do anything about. Into this crack is driven the wedge of melodrama, understood here as the consequence of the unknowably singular malign. Characters in the stories are always telling Faith, something of an author-surrogate, to shut up and listen. Narrative optimism collides with their belief in enemies. She argues that no one has tried good sense. "It hasn't been built up or experimented with sufficiently." Against this argument, Jack, the narrator's friend in "The Immigrant Story," tells a horrific tale of European famine and terror that leaves the remnant family huddled against a perpetual darkness.

> They are sitting at the edge of their chairs. He's leaning forward reading to her in that old bulb light. Sometimes she smiles just a little. Then he puts the paper down and takes both her hands in his as though they needed warmth. He continues to read. Just beyond the table and their heads, there is the darkness of the kitchen, the bedroom, the dining room, the shadowy darkness where as a child I ate my supper, did my homework and went to bed.

This passage, with its thick chordal resonances of sorrow, could come out of Malamud or Singer or any writer familiarly acquainted with grief. To my ear it bears witness to the implacable furies trailing behind the Holocaust. This passage is hushed, and the narrator's voice does not return when it's over. As in Chekhov, a frame is found for the sorrow, but the darkness—all but allegorical in this passage—is a chiaroscuro halo, almost sentient, and so strong that Jack's Marxist and Freudian thinking can't dispel it. We are in the presence of an *absolute* mood. Although the narrator says that the "whole world ought to be opposed to Europe," her voice sounds comic and American-optimist by comparison.

The terror of the world against the innocent comes forward out of the obscurity in another story in *Enormous Changes* called "The Little Girl." This is not a story that admirers of Paley's fiction tend to remember. The story is never anthologized and did not appear in any magazine before appearing in the book. In its way, the story is what I would call an example of melodramatic realism. No gestures are made to exaggerate terror in it, and there's no wallowing or gloating in violence. All the same, the mysteriousness—the inexplicability—of inflicted pain is visible everywhere in it.

A man named Charlie tells the story. It's mostly about his friend Carter. Carter asks Charlie if he can use Charlie's apartment; he's going to have company later on. Charlie has been picking up white girls in the park—both men are African American—girls described as "soft yellow-haired baby chicks." Charlie goes on to witness and to tell how Charlie picks up "this child . . . just straggling along." She says she's eighteen but "that was a lie and Carter knew it, I believe . . . [a] grown man got to use his sense."

Charlie reconstructs what then happens from what he imagines and from what Carter tells him. Carter and the girl get to the apartment. The girl is disappointed by the look of things. Carter gets violent with her, and when he's finished, and she's "tore up some . . . sniffling and that blood spreading around her," he leaves. As he leaves, another man, Angie Emporiore, is standing in the doorway, looking on, about to take advantage of the situation.

The girl's body is found at the bottom of the window's airshaft, "every bone between her knee and her rib cage broken, splintered." She has been assaulted with a blunt instrument and bitten and torn up.

Charlie's speculation ends the story. He thinks that perhaps she wasn't thrown through the window; she jumped. And the reason she jumped is that she has been visited by absolute horror. It's stated with a bedeviled, sideways tact.

> Maybe she pull herself the way she was, crumpled, to that open window. She was tore up, she must of thought she was gutted inside her skin. She must of been in a horror what she got to remember—what her folks would see. Her life look to be disgusting like a squashed fish, so what she did: she made up some power somehow and raise herself up that windowsill and hook herself onto it and then what I see, she just topple herself out. That what I think right now.

Like the shadows around Jack's parents in "The Immigrant Story," the "horror what she got to remember" is what the story insists on. It's a story about shock, and shock defeats most of our good intentions and our good sense. Paley does not include the word "horror" easily or casually in her fiction, and its appearance here takes us back to the problem of singularity. As often as I have taught *Enormous Changes at the Last Minute* to undergraduate and adult classes, I have never found a group willing to talk about this story. They have nothing to say about what happens in it, or else they simply refuse, out of some combination of good sense, shyness, and gloom, to discuss it. Collective clamming-up is the rule, not the exception. "The Little Girl" defeats reasoned discourse, puts a limit on speech, renders the observer as silent or as stuttering as Billy Budd. The story stands in every respect against whatever the reader or even the characters in the story might wish. No evil is desired, it seems, by Charlie or Carter or Angie or even the girl, but it's a precipitate of their actions. It erupts in the meeting of half-innocent curiosity, racism, sex, and poverty. Its visible causes are both adequate *and* insufficient.

The story is a mulling, a monologue, as many of Paley's stories are. Charlie's monologue is a forcing-into-fiction of what would rather be an unformulated nightmare. What's happened is so horrible that Charlie can't stop imagining it, probably can't stop talking about, but there is no place for the imagination here, or any role for it to play. Charlie is forced to circle around and around the scene of action in order to find either an explanation or something for the mind to do, a place for it to be. *Carter cannot have thrown the little girl out of the window. Maybe she threw herself out.* But both possibilities are almost equally unbearable, except that in Charlie's version of the events, the second case, the little girl "made up some power somehow."

Out of the telling of the story, the victim makes up some power. That seems the only possible addition to the narrated events that acts to counter the relentless movement toward calamity, the brute facts of pain and violent death. Against these horrors stands the smallest courage. This story (despite what the father says in "Conversation with My Father") does manage to look tragedy in the face. If the word "tragedy" sounds a bit high-minded for "The Little Girl," the events nevertheless justify its common associations. The social and personal trauma that

Charlie imagines and, in remembering and speaking, reenacts, is the singularity that calls forth the repetitive telling of a traumatic event. This is what both Freud and Walter Benjamin have noticed about trauma. The activity of telling the story serves to air rather than to erase the wound.

Unlike most of Paley's other stories, "The Little Girl" has no charm or breeziness. Its actions occur as if on a chain or inside a cage. The customary voice of the Paley-narrator is absent from it, vacated. Charlie is enacting a monologue in which the dead girl, now forever torn and damaged, speaks. We are in the place of the dead, in Hell. That place is where the reader is moved to, in this eight-page story: into the last living setting of the hapless unnamed dead girl brought to fictional life in Charlie's compulsive telling. The Paley narrator is not speaking anywhere in this story but is almost audibly listening.

The story does not give up on politics. Its events do not argue for futility or guarantee betterment. Maybe they are a precondition for politics. Certainly they call forth the ancient emotions of pity and terror. All the same, to look this situation "in the face," as the doctor-father says, calls forth a form of horror that is, to use an adjective from "Heart of Darkness," inscrutable.

In an interview first printed in 1965, Orson Welles was asked about the relation of tragedy and melodrama, and Welles replied that in the Anglo-Saxon cultural universe, no one had succeeded in separating the two. "Shakespeare," he says, "never arrived at it." He went on to say, "In my cultural tradition, tragedy cannot escape from melodrama. . . . melodrama is always inherent in the Anglo-Saxon cultural universe." These statements of course say a great deal about Welles. But in distinguishing

English tragedy from, say, the tragedies of Racine, Welles makes a point that may be wrong but is certainly not stupid. In the Anglo-Saxon tradition, melodrama for better or worse usually provides the structure for thinking about misfortune.

A distaste for melodrama in any form is probably a sign of great good luck.

A separate essay might be written on the evidence of melodramatic elements in Romantic and late Modernist poetry from Blake through Coleridge and Keats, down to Robert Frost and from there to the next generation of Lowell, Roethke, and Plath, and, among current poets, Stanley Kunitz, Sharon Olds, Frank Bidart, Amiri Baraka, and, at times, Adrienne Rich. Each of them has a sense of being haunted by dualities and demons, the hounds barking in the distance.

The stubbornness of melodrama, its refusal to go away. Its interest in panic and flight, the obscurity of the opposition, and solitary stands against darkness. The limitations it places on the power of intelligence to enlighten. The stain that won't go away. The persistent observation that most of us are unlucky. That suffering is inevitable but pleasure fleeting. Its glorious but rare sense of humor. "[S]piritual life," as Henry James, Sr., wrote to his sons, "is a subdued forest where the wolf howls. . . ." Its traumas. Its usually ineffective doctors and therapists.

"And you know what else, Doctor?" asks Midge, in Hitchcock's *Vertigo*. "I don't think Mozart's going to help at all."

Notes

Walter Benjamin, "On Some Motifs in Baudelaire," in *Illuminations*. Edited by Hannah Arendt, translated by Harry Zohn (New York: Schocken Books, 1969).

Peter Brooks, *The Melodramatic Imagination* (New York: Columbia University Press, 1985).

Friedrich Nietzsche, *The Case of Wagner.* Translated by Walter Kaufmann (New York: Vintage, 1965).

Martha Vicinus, "'Helpless and Unfriended': Nineteenth-Century Domestic Melodrama." *New Literary History* (Autumn 1981): 127–143.

The Donald Barthelme Blues

The same day that a friend called with the news that Donald Barthelme had died, a freight train derailed outside Freeland, Michigan. Among the cars that went off the tracks were several chemical tankers, some of which spilled and caught fire. Dow Chemical was (and still is) reluctant to name these chemicals, but one of them was identified as chlorosilene. When chlorosilene catches fire, as it did in this case, it turns into hydrochloric acid. Upon being asked about the physical hazards to neighbors and onlookers near the fire, a company representative, interviewed on Michigan Public Radio, said, "Well, there's been some physical reactions, yes, certainly. Especially in the area of nausea, vomiting-type thing."

The area of nausea, vomiting-type thing: This area, familiar to us all, where bad taste, hilarity, fake authority, and cliché seem to collide, was Donald Barthelme's special kingdom. "I have a few new marvels here I'd like to discuss with you just briefly," says the chief engineer in "Report." "Consider for instance the area of realtime online computer-controlled wish evaporation." Like his creation Hokie Mokie, the King of Jazz, no one could top Barthelme at deadpan riffs like these—these collages built

157

from castoff verbal junk—and imitation was beside the point, because the work was not a compendium of stylistic tics but grew out of—has anyone bothered to say this?—a spiritual enterprise owned up to in the work, a last stay against the forces of wish evaporation. Comedy is partly the art of collage, of planned incongruity—the Three Stooges as brain surgeons, King Kong as an adjunct professor of art history—and Barthelme was a master tailor of these ill-fitting suits in which our culture likes to dress itself. A yoking of the virtuosic-articulate with the flat banal; an effort to preserve wishes, and certain kinds of longings, in the face of clichés; not innocence, but a watchful clarity, even an effort to preserve the monstrousness of Being itself: All these difficult ambitions seemed to be part of the scheme. The work was a comfort, in the way the blues are a comfort, in its refusal to buy stock in the official Happiness Project, in its loyalty to "inappropriate longings," a phrase whose ironic positive side he particularly valued.

As an undergraduate I was taught that when a writer starts a story, s/he must begin with *a character,* an active, preferably vivid, ideally sympathetic, character. It takes a bit of time to see that stories don't in fact begin with characters, not from here, at least, not from behind this keyboard. They begin with words, one word after another. It seems doltish to point this out, but in Donald Barthelme's fiction, that's where the project begins: with the stress first on the language, the medium, and then on the problem of who owns it. Who does own language? I can evade the question by saying that no one does; it is just out there, part of the culture. But Barthelme did not practice this evasion. In his stories, all kinds of disreputable people claim to own both language and its means of distribution. They invent instant clichés that they want you to buy and use; they want you to join and submit to their formulas. Invariably, they are selling something that can only be sold if they trash up the language first. They are lively practitioners of a black art, these commodifiers, and Barthelme's stories don't mind saying so.

Barthelme's characters inhabit not the prison-house of language, but the prison-house of official cliché—which is not the same thing as saying "Fine" when someone asks how you are but is more a processing of statements into the professional formulas usually called jargon, like the analyst's transformation of Susan's statement (in "The Sandman") that she wants to buy a piano into, "She wishes to terminate the analysis and escape into the piano." The narrator, Susan's boyfriend and a slightly irritable opponent of normative psychotherapy, observes that the analyst is methodologically horse-blindered: "The one thing you cannot consider, by the nature of your training and of the discipline itself, is that she really might want to terminate the analysis and buy a piano."

What *are* the conditions under which we lose the ability to know what we want? And what are the exact words for longing? Most of the words we have are not the words for what we really want. "What we really want in this world, we can't have" ("The Ed Sullivan Show"). There is a certain stranded quality to the Barthelme protagonist, sitting in an easy chair at twilight with eleven martinis lined up in soldierly array. A fastidiousness, this is, and a humor about the shipwrecked condition, the orphaned longings, and something like an investigation of the possibilities inherent in melancholy. The heroes and heroines in this fiction are the not-joiners, the *non serviam* types, like Cecelia in "A City of Churches," who has come to Prester to open a car-rental office. Mr. Phillips guides her around. It turns out that in Prester everyone lives in a church of one kind or another, "the church of their choice." Mr. Phillips asks Cecelia what denomination she is: "Cecelia was silent. The truth was, she wasn't anything." She tells him, however, that she can will her dreams. What dreams? "'Mostly sexual things,' she said. She was not afraid of him." Mr. Phillips admits to a certain discontent with Prester, despite the town's perfection. "I'll dream the Secret," Cecelia says. "You'll be sorry."

Notice the capitalization of the word *secret*. Our secrets might be the last places where we have hidden ourselves away, where we are still upper-case. Susan wants her piano; Cecelia wants her dreams; and the Phantom of the Opera resists the operation that would, as we might say now, *renormalize* him. All any of these heroes would have to do to be renormalized is trade in their desires for rooms furnished with comfortable clichés: nice wing chairs, plastic slipcovers. The Phantom's friend waits, patiently, "until the hot meat of romance is cooled by the dull gravy of common sense once more." That's a long time, if you're loyal to your desires.

The price one pays for being loyal to certain kinds of anomalies is typically melancholy or acedia. Barthelme's fiction asserts that one of the first loyalties serious people give up in the theater of adulthood is a claim upon what they actually want. Of course, other desires are available, and can be acquired, but they are curious grafts, what other people want you to want— not desires so much as temptations, desires-of-convenience. Barthelme's stories are obviously and constantly about such temptations, which might itself be called the temptation to become unconscious and let others program your yearnings. The stories exude an almost religious seriousness about this subject; although they are not pious, they do move obsessively around ethical-theological quandaries. A good deal of reading about religion is made visible in them. The Barthelmean character is tempted not by ordinary sins but by the ordinary itself. Does God care about adultery? Sins generally? "You think about this staggering concept, the mind of God, and then you think He's sitting around worrying about this guy and this woman at the Beechnut Travelodge? I think not." *(Paradise)*.

It wasn't activities like adultery that caught Barthelme's attention, but the inclination to disown one's wishes and to give in to the omnipresence of the Universal Banal. Barthelme was not a snob in this respect; plain common pleasures—food, sex, Fleetwood Mac, John Ford movies, dull days at home—find themselves celebrated (however mildly) in his pages; ordinary pleasures are all right if that is what you really want. But no, the problem is not the banal as such but banality's hope that you will dumbfoundedly join in its program, spend yourself in it: That's the problem. In Barthelme a saint is tempted not by sin but by life in the suburbs: "St. Anthony's major temptation, in terms of his living here, was maybe this: ordinary life." ("The Temptation of St. Anthony"). People want to see his apartment; they want to look at the carpet from Kaufman's, and the bedroom. How might a Saint resist the ordinary?

A simple question, calling forth slyly complicated answers. One begins by talking about deserts (where the Saint goes), grottos, the stony home of the grotesque. In a catalogue commentary on a Sherrie Levine exhibit, Barthelme put it this way:

> Where does desire go? Always a traveling salesperson, desire goes hounding off into the trees, frequently, without direction from its putative master or mistress. This is tragic and comic at the same time. I should, in a well-ordered world, marry the intellectual hero my wicked uncle has selected for me. Instead I run off with William of Ockham or Daffy Duck.

William of Ockham or Daffy Duck: Yes, the true object of your desire quite often looks and sounds a bit, well, bizarre, and hard to introduce to your wicked uncle. The more bizarre the object, the more Barthelme seems to like it. There is a pleasant sideshow quality, a circus element, to the spectacle of desire. It generates dwarfs and witches *(Snow White),* a son manqué (eight feet tall and wearing "a serape woven out of two hundred transistor radios" in "The Dolt"), monsters, and impossibly beautiful women. It's as if longing generates out of itself, as Susan Stewart has argued in her book on the subject, narratives of the gigantic and tiny, narratives of altered proportion: There is the dead father, that huge living corpse of origination, being dragged around by the bickering sons; there are the zombies, spouting their death-in-life clichés; there is King Kong, already alluded to, the adjunct professor of art history at Rutgers. Big and little: Figures of all sizes and shapes have their moment in the most highly invented sentences grammar and sense permit. This sideshow resides very comfortably, too, in the short-story form, a haven, as Frank O'Connor has claimed, for the otherwise disappeared, all the everyone-elses who fall between the cracks of the more official forms, such as the novel and the sonnet.

Behind this cultivation of the beautiful grotesque, this show-and-tell of the alien wish, a certain weariness is sometimes apparent. One is after all confronted by the banal in the midst of the weird; there is also that terrible moment familiar to all members of the avant-garde when the weird *becomes* the banal. "Some things appear to be wonders in the beginning, but when you become familiar with them, are not wonderful at all. Sometimes a seventy-five-foot highly paid cacodemon will raise only the tiniest *frisson.* Some of us have even thought of folding the show—closing it down." ("The Flight of Pigeons from the Palace").

What is the secret name of this weariness? At first it is called irony, and then acedia.

Under the powerful microscope of post-structuralist neo-

Marxist semiotically based hyphen-using critical theory,
Barthelme's fiction at first seems to be all about cultural junk,
verbal junk, "the leading edge of the trash phenomenon," and
about the way structures of meaning, let loose from the objects
they're supposed to represent, are pasted onto something else
(the Campbell's Pork-and-Beans labels on my necktie; Elvis's
Jailhouse Rock on dinner plates from the Franklin Mint; the
Batman label on sandwiches). Words go wild. They are set free
from the house of correction and have a party ("Bone Bubbles")
or, freed up like a chatty aunt off her medication, go on and on
("Sentence"). For a time in the early seventies, Barthelme and
John Ashbery seemed to be operating similar circuses in different parts of town. This period included the moment of greatest academic interest in Barthelme's work; critics had much to
say about the mechanisms of meaning in the fiction, about the
arbitrariness of the sign and the problems of language. The defamiliarization in the work matched the defamiliarization of
American social life. But semiotics and fragments are not the
essential subjects of these stories. I'm not sure how often it has
been noticed that Barthelme's imagery, cast of characters, and
preoccupations are drawn from religious sources. Who is the
dead father in *The Dead Father*? The father and The Father. In
"City Life," Ramona gives birth to Sam; it's a virgin birth. Angels,
in their current earthly diminished lives, have their say in "On
Angels." Kierkegaard is invoked several times. Such maneuver-
ing has an element of travesty in it, a playing around with the
broken relics of religious iconography and meaning-creation;
but religion appears so often and with such odd sideways intensity that it signals a persistent curiosity about the Absolute and
some of its elements as authenticity (in post-structuralist thinking, a completely discredited category).

   In Barthelme's early stories, modern culture is gleefully and

relentlessly unmasked: engineers, doctors, politicians, news-
papers, television quiz shows, and the plastic assembled-with-
glue language they use. There is a certain violence in the ripping
off of the masks here, a ferocity that produces a prose poetry
(Barthelme probably would have hated the term) of rage and
clarity. Lines often quoted from the first paragraph of "The
Indian Uprising" hit this note and sustain it: "People were trying to understand. I spoke to Sylvia. 'Do you think this is a good
life?' The table held apples, books, long-playing records. She
looked up. 'No.'"

These early stories sometimes seem to demonstrate that the
serious world is about as well constructed as a puppet show; it is
certainly no more real. All experience gives way to representation. You pull back the pretense: another pretense. Pictures give
way to pictures, acts to acts. It's unhinging, the metaphysics of
the onionskin giving way to nothing: The wisps and whiffs of
frenzy I hear in *Come Back, Dr. Caligari, Unspeakable Practices,
Unnatural Acts,* and *City Life* strike me as sounds made by someone reaching for the irreducibly real but coming up with fistfuls
of sand—or an empire of signs, themselves nauseating and re-
vealing of nothing. Knowing—as the Barthelmean narrator
knows so well—that this reaching, this frenzy, and this sand are
commonplaces in the history of twentieth-century spiritual-
critical life is no solace. What good is it to know that your
metaphysical nausea, which you suffer from daily, has been experienced before and expressed very well by Mallarmé, Sartre,
and the others? As the stories themselves say, "No good at all!"

Starting with "Kierkegaard Unfair to Schlegel," in *City Life*
and then intermittently throughout the other books, Barthelme
seemed to be setting himself a challenge to go beyond this un-
masking process—a process that would, if continued indefinitely,
have yielded up wacky but tedious self-repeating satires, or ex-

ercises in dry malice. The nature of this challenge is not easy
to state discursively, but it may be at the center of any life that
is simultaneously mindful and bourgeois (if in fact those two
categories can be placed next to each other). We can call it, in
honor of one of its first diagnosticians, the Chekhov problem,
which goes something like this: What does one do, do actively,
with one's honest revulsion and disgust with the cruelties, lies,
and deceptions of middle-class life? Chekhov's response to this
challenge—this is a gross oversimplification—is to show that,
hidden under the outward mimes of character there lies the
substance of real character, a kind of essence. Something genuine sooner or later will show itself; all we need do is wait, observe, and hold onto those moments when they arrive. In this
way, weariness and cynicism are kept at arm's length. Because
no character can be wholly co-opted by any system, some par-
ticle of the genuine will emerge at some point.

This solution, if one can call it that, was closed to Barthelme
almost from the beginning. Either he did not believe in character in this sense (one cannot imagine him using so square a
phrase as "real character underneath"), or he had no feel for it
as a writer. As a result his characters tend toward allegory and
stylization. Exceptions exist, notably in the Bishop stories, but
they are few. It is not so much that the characters in Barthelme's
fiction are unreal but that they seem to have been constructed
more out of preexisting emotions than out of motivations, a
more common writerly starting point. In any case, without the
solution of character, we are back at the original problem of what
to do after all the lies have been exposed. And of course we are
still enjoying the unreflecting privileges of middle-class life.

This far from trivial problem exists only if you assume that
middle-class American life does carry with it a gnawing burden of guilt. I think I could argue that a significant number of

the strategies of contemporary American "serious" fiction are maneuvers for dealing with the issue of middle-class guilt. One possibility is to handle it more or less as Chekhov did. Another, also very common, is the strategy of cynicism, enjoying the benefits of middle-class life while holding oneself slightly above it. A third response, almost always characterized as "toughness," has been a part of American culture for at least a century. Toughness is the obverse side of sentimentality, fighting against and reflecting it all at the same time. It is the poetry of denial. What it refuses to give to character it lavishes on its prose, which typically is highly stylized and self-regarding. The idea is to withhold expressions of human sympathy—because they seem "weak" and because they capitulate to a false order of experience. Hemingway is the great bard of this mode, saying in effect I-may-be-here-but-I'm-not-really-part-of-this-scene. Obviously, cynicism and toughness may be easily combined as strategies. They carry with them a certain feeling for hermit life, for withholding, and for clipped sentences, oracular statements, and derailed ordinary language. However, the toughness mode is crabbed and repetitious, qualities that Barthelme never sought. He invented situations and sentences: I'd like to quote page after page of them, hair-raising for their sheer sound, their surprises and elaborations. Their shine. No: Toughness, the metaphysics of the hermit crab, was not enough.

Which returns us to the problem of cynicism, which does not seem an adequate response to the problem of being located inside conflicting desires, of being the very person one does not want to be. Cynicism and its spiritual second-cousin, irony, are regular combatants in Barthelme's stories, but there is something wrong with both of them; the stories work hard to disclose what it is. For one thing, cynicism is hypocritical: It enjoys what it claims to despise. It is happy in its unhappy con-

sciousness. It understands the destructiveness of its own pleasures but does nothing to stop it. It is enlightened about its own
moral condition. It will agree to any accusation made against it.
World-weariness is its poetry. Growing out of snobbery, its only
pleasure is manipulation. Cynicism is irony that has moved
into a condition of institutional power; cynicism and power
have a tendency to breed each other. But Barthelme's stories—
especially the early ones and the novel *Snow White*—typically
struggle against institutional cynicism and the language employed in its cause. To use a phrase by the German philosopher Peter Sloterdijk, employed in another context, these are
"études in the higher banalities." Far from being an exercise in
cynicism, the narrative voice in Barthelme consistently attacks
cynicism—the cynicism of official institutional spokespersons.
But the weapon that comes most readily to hand is irony, which
creates the (as Barthelme might say) *interesting* struggle and
tension in his writing.

The nature of the problem, if you simultaneously feel guilty
and disgusted by the progress of modern culture, is the temptation to become a snob, to join a like-minded coterie of people
with good taste who define themselves by an awareness of all the
vulgarities they do not perform. Or you can become a hermit
like Saint Anthony, benefiting from the culture while pretending not to live in it. Viewed unsympathetically, this is a central impulse in Modernism, one of its worst errors. Barthelme's
fiction never makes this error: It challenges readers but never
insults them or pretends to instruct them from an angle higher
than their own. It disclaims righteousness. "The Party" concludes by asking: "Is it really important to know that this movie
is fine, and that one terrible, and to talk intelligently about the
difference? Wonderful elegance! No good at all!"

At this point, the really astonishing difficulties of Barthelme's project start to become apparent. Exiled from character-drawing, and in the midst of (one might almost say "drowning in") cultural sign-systems, most of which are duplicitous, the Barthelmean narrator must struggle simply in order to find a location, a place to stand and speak that is not so far inside the culture that it replicates its falseness and lies, and not so far outside that it becomes cold, snobby, or self-righteous. This is a problem not just for writers but for anyone who lives in a powerful and culturally dominant country. And it is not an issue that anyone finally "solves." Writers must devise strategies for dealing with it, some of which are more effective than others. Some are distracting—and Barthelme's work is very high, one might almost say intoxicated, with distractions—while also presenting roads and avenues, certain kinds of metaphorical paths for action. And they do so with a good deal of warmth—as in the ending of "Daumier," where Celeste is in the kitchen, making a *daube,* and the narrator says he will go in to watch her. The story ends with two sentences that, in their quietness, modesty, and precision, have always moved me. "The self cannot be escaped, but it can be, with ingenuity and hard work, distracted. There are always openings, if you can find them, there is always something to do."

One word for this technique is *forbearance.* Starting with the stories in *City Life,* we move onto a thematic ground governed by a feeling where piano music instead of analysis might be possible, where "little dances of suggestion and fear" might be staged: "These dances constitute an invitation of unmistakable import—an invitation which, if accepted, leads down many muddy roads. I accepted. What was the alternative?" ("City Life"). Odd, the fastidious articulation of these feelings, their insistence on the possibility of continued action. And beautiful, the playing with children, the turning to childhood, in two late stories, "Chablis" and "The Baby."

As for religion: Can one discard its content and still admire its interest in, perhaps its necessary commitment to, the issue of where one places oneself in relation to one's own experiences? This is exactly the question that arises in two of Barthelme's most interesting stories, "Kierkegaard Unfair to Schlegel" and "January" (the last story in *Forty Stories* and therefore something of a curtain speech). In both stories we are in the presence of a ghostly sort of interview, considerably more ghostly in the Kierkegaard story, which gives the sense of an internal quarrel or an interview between two spirit entities.

Characters named Q. and A., Question and Answer, argue in "Kierkegaard Unfair to Schlegel," with Q. being particularly annoyed by A.'s inability to get enthusiastic about "our machines": "You've withheld your enthusiasm, that's damaging. . . ." Something like the problem of cynicism arises here, the question of spiritual snobbery. A. answers by discussing irony, which he uses in conjunction with political activism:

> I participate. I make demands, sign newspaper advertisements,
> vote. I make small campaign contributions to the candidate
> of my choice and turn my irony against the others. But I ac-
> complish nothing. I march, it's ludicrous.

This sense of self-irony leads into a discussion of Kierkegaard and his analysis of irony as a magical power that confers upon its user a "negative freedom." When irony is directed against the whole of existence, the result, says Kierkegaard, is "estrangement and poetry"—a poetry that "opens up a higher actuality, expands and transfigures the imperfect into the perfect, and thereby softens and mitigates the deep pain which would darken and obscure all things." Thus Kierkegaard. Unfortunately, this variety of poetry does not reconcile one to the world but produces an animosity to the world:

A. But I love my irony.

Q. Does it give you pleasure?

A. A poor . . . a rather unsatisfactory. . . .

Q. The unavoidable tendency of everything particular to emphasize its own particularity.

A. Yes.

If Barthelme were the kind of ironist described by Kierkegaard, the sort who turns his irony upon the "whole of existence," then he would be tracking Beckett in pursuit of an absolute negativity, thinking directed against being itself. Or he would be following William Gass into a principality built out of the toothpicks and straw of words. But although this irony has the virtue of purity, it can in no way account for the pleasures we consciously enjoy in Barthelme's fiction. What is their ultimate source?

Answering this question seems to me the task Barthelme set himself in his novel *Paradise,* published in 1986. If it is about anything, this book is about pleasures, even beatitude: the pleasure of sex and the friendship it can produce; the pleasure of making and building (its protagonist, Simon, is an architect); the pleasure—unbelievable to imagine this in the early books—of improving the world. The tone of this book, in its mixture of fantasy, high comedy, and caring, is close to blessedness. Barthelme of course gives his usual warnings about stupid optimism:

> Simon wanted very much to be a hearty, optimistic American, like the President, but on the other hand did not trust hearty, optimistic Americans, like the President. He had considered the possibility that the President . . . was not really hearty and optimistic but rather a gloomy, obsessed man.

Because the fantasy in this story—a single man living with three beautiful women—is so stylized, the imaginative force

seems to move from the specific situation to the nature of the
lineaments of gratified desire. The book is therefore about happiness. It is as if Barthelme were saying that we must try to
imagine happiness. This book is one version of it. Happiness,
in these times, may be the last frontier of the imagination, the
most difficult challenge of all. But if happiness cannot be imagined, if alienation cannot be balmed at the source, then truly
one might as well do nothing, or simply drift toward death. Near
the end of *Paradise,* Barthelme argues that our desires inhabit
and inspirit us:

> Simon flew to North Carolina to inspect a job he'd done in
> Winston-Salem, a hospital. The construction was quite good
> and he found little to complain of. He admired the fenestra-
> tion, done by his own hand. He spent an agreeable night in
> a Ramada Inn and flew back the next day. His seatmate was
> a young German woman on her way to Frankfurt. She was
> six months pregnant, she said, and her husband, an Army
> sergeant in Chemical Warfare, had found a new girl friend,
> was divorcing her. She had spent two years at Benning, loved
> America, spoke with what seemed to Simon a Texas accent.
> Her father was dead and her mother operated a candy store in
> Frankfurt. They talked about pregnancy and delivery, about
> how much wine she allowed herself, whether aspirin was in
> fact a danger to the baby, and how both of her brothers-in-law
> had been born in taxis. She was amazingly cheerful given the
> circumstances and told him that the Russians were going to
> attempt to take over Mexico next. We had neglected Mexico,
> she said.
>   Over the Atlantic on the long approach to Kennedy Simon
> saw a hundred miles of garbage in the water, from the air
> white floating scruff. The water became agitated at points
> as fish attacked the garbage and Simon turned his mind to
> compaction. When they landed he kissed the German woman

goodbye and told her that although she probably didn't feel very lucky at the moment, she was very lucky.

That's beautiful. The balance is miraculous. Everything that is—including abandonment, garbage, ecological decay—is held in equilibrium with what is possible: delivery, compaction. There is always something to do. The style is also beautiful, because of all the hurricanes Barthelme has traveled through in order to formulate this difficult calm. The book ends up radiating not a sense of peacefulness but a sense of high intellectual and spiritual comedy, a form of art characteristic of late middle and old age.

"January" concludes Barthelme's final collection, *Forty Stories*. The first month. This piece (*is* it a story? of what sort?) presents an interview with theologian Thomas Brecker, whose dissertation was written in the forties on the subject of acedia:

> The thesis was that acedia is a turning toward something rather than, as it's commonly conceived of, a turning away from something. I argued that acedia is a positive reaction to extraordinary demand, for example, the demand that one embrace the *good news* and become one with the mystical body of Christ. . . . Acedia is often conceived of as a kind of sullenness in the face of existence; I tried to locate its positive features. For example, it precludes certain kinds of madness, crowd mania, it precludes a certain kind of error. You're not an enthusiast and therefore you don't go out and join a lynch mob—rather you languish on a couch with your head in your hands.

Brecker goes on to talk about the healing power of absolution, its ability to create new directions. He thinks about his own death, "I hate to abandon my children," and concludes the story this way:

The point of my career is perhaps how little I achieved. We speak of someone as having had "a long career" and that's usually taken to be admiring, but what if it's thirty-five years of persistence in error? I don't know what value to place on what I've done, perhaps none at all is right. If I'd done something with soybeans, been able to increase the yield of an acre of soybeans, then I'd know I'd done something. I can't say that.

Barthelme's last collection of stories ends here, in a perfectly serious tone of modesty, not to say humility. "I was trying," Brecker says, "to stake out a position for the uncommitted which still, at the same time, had something to do with religion." It would be incorrect to say that Barthelme, the chronicler of word-nausea, had mellowed into the drabness of total sincerity. What actually seems to have emerged toward the end is both more interesting and more complicated: a kind of tenderness toward existence, isolated from the junk of culture through which it is commonly viewed. Although still surrounded by intellectual defenses, and therefore still enveloped and distracted, these later stories are generous; almost miraculously they transform metaphysical irony into caring watchfulness. Giving up finally *does* turn into giving over. Although it is not typically American to have a second act in one's career, and then a third, and even a fourth, Barthelme had them. And despite what was sometimes said against him, he did not repeat himself, did not endlessly replay the old tricks. He found new tricks, and then, toward the end, discarded most of them. How rare, also, in America, to see writing develop into such variety and generosity! Almost unheard-of. Almost unseen.

Stillness

*My work is rooted in silence. It grows out of deep
beds of contemplation, where words, which are living
things, can form and re-form into new wholes.
What is visible, the finished books, are underpinned
by the fertility of uncounted hours. A writer has no
use for the clock. A writer lives in an infinity of days,
time without end, ploughed under.*

*It is sometimes necessary to be silent for months
before the central image of a book can occur.*
—Jeanette Winterson, *Art Objects*

It's late at night, and you are quarreling with someone on the telephone, long distance. You have reached a stalemate of sorts, where nothing remains to be said. You cannot hang up. But you cannot say anything more. So you remain on the line. Neither of you utters a word. A moment like this stirs the air with an odd and indefinable feeling. It is not like the silence after a quarrel in a room, because AT&T is going to bill you (or the other person) for this silence. This gap—this emotional and techno-logical emptiness—is literally going to cost you.

In the days before fiber-optic technology, these moments also happened to put you into the wash of background trans-mission noise. Behind your mutual silence in the foreground came the faraway hiss and gurgle of the wires. Sometimes, distantly, you could hear other conversations. Straining not to speak yourself, you might end up eavesdropping on someone's random casual happiness. You might hear laughter, laughter hundreds of miles away, still faintly audible.

The hiss and gurgle and the laughter are the markers of time moving through stillness.

In one of his film reviews, James Agee refers to "expressive air-pockets of dead silence." The reference is to intentional gaps in the dialogue of Alfred Hitchcock's *Notorious*.

Expressive air-pockets of dead silence. They are theatrical, and relatively easy to manage on film or on stage (think of Pinter). But how does anyone get them into fiction, where the flow of words must continue line by line, page by page, until the whole thing stops?

We often think of silence as being a blank, a null set, or of all silences being similar, expressing the same thing, the same nothing. We may not actually need John Cage, however, to show us that silence is an intensifier—that it strengthens whatever stands on either side of it. Directed in this way, silence takes on a different emotion, a different color, for whatever it flows through or flows between.

What's remarkable is the degree to which Americans have distrusted silence and its parent condition, stillness. In this country, silence is often associated with madness, mooncalfing, woolgathering, laziness, hostility, and stupidity. Stillness is regularly associated with death. The distrust of silence and stillness comes to us as a form of muddleheaded late-Puritanism, which looks upon idle hands as the devil's playground, and silence, like Hester Prynne's silence, as privatized rebellion, a refusal to join the team.

The daydreaming child, or daydreaming adult, is usually an object of contempt or therapy. Vitality in our culture, by contrast, has everything to do with speed and talk. In Postmodernism, speed and information, combined through data processing, have moved into cyberspace. It is no wonder that the metaphor of the superhighway has stuck and has become an instant international cliché. But when speed is made to be the defining feature of *action*, violence is usually not far away, violence defined here as the loss of control under conditions of great velocity. Violence, unlike daydreaming, is not—this is worth our attention—an object of contempt. Fear, perhaps, but not contempt.

Our fascination with violence is equal to our fascination with data processing; they are two coins in the same pocket.

What conceivable relation is there between narrative violence and data processing? Speed, for one thing, and the necessity of coping with information that may be both dangerous and evanescent. People who work all day at computers often get keyed up, tense, and anxious because of the speed of the information flow. It does not seem to me that a day spent reading from pages has the same effect because the information flows at a different rate. On computers, information seems to move at great speed because users sit still in front of a screen. In this century, we have all learned to sit still in front of screens: movie and TV screens, computer screens, windshield/windscreens. As we sit still in front of these screens, we often witness representations of great violence. Stillness on one side, violence or speed on the other. People who can't sit still in front of these screens are said to have another twentieth-century invention, an affliction called attention deficit disorder.

Velocity understood in relation to action and language has been, throughout this century, one of those ideological headaches that will not go away. The peculiar and immeasurable speed of language as it carries information is a special problem of the twentieth century, because we are being bombarded by information at a rate unknown to previous eras, information produced by the forces of industrialization and urbanization, and the mass production of commodities and populations. The resulting data-nausea and information sickness are probably unique, at least on a mass scale, to our time.

Information sickness has lately become a concern for anyone who aspires to write fiction. Fiction involves a conversion: a conversion of information into experience. In the early part of this century, the critic Walter Benjamin worried over the displacement of experience by information: Excessive quantities of information in daily life, he thought, would block the experience of being transported by the storyteller. When that happens, the reader or the listener gets stuck at the level of data. Everything becomes discursive, with no sense of what Gertrude Stein later called "the excitement of contemporariness," the transformation of information into the experience of story.

With her customary goofy and cryptic insight, Gertrude Stein noticed that something was happening to the experience of time in the reading of fiction after the turn of the century. In her essay "How Writing Is Written," published in 1935, she observes that in the twentieth century, events "have lost their interest for people." Events, she says, have become like syrup.

This is a curious idea. It suggests that action, in fiction, has been drained of some intrinsic interest. We still need action, of course, but when we have it in front of us we don't notice it as much as readers did in previous centuries. In this sense, action is like the syrup just referred to, or a drug. If you are a cigarette smoker, you know what it is like to need a cigarette when you don't have one, yet not even notice when you light up and actually begin smoking. The craving is often sharper than the satisfaction. Action, as Gertrude Stein understood, has turned into just this kind of narcotic. You don't get *interested* in a narcotic; you just need it. Needing something is not the same thing as being interested in the thing itself.

This is an idea at the center of certain forms of Modernism. There is a branch of Modernism that distrusts all things in motion and trusts all things that are still. Gertrude Stein said that soldiers standing around on street corners during and after World War I, doing nothing much, were more interesting to people than when the soldiers went over the top. Although she does not say so in her essay, and certainly would not have said so, *A Farewell to Arms*—which is after all a love story with World War I somewhere there in the background—continues to be read when novels about trench warfare have disappeared.

This idea, that events have become like a syrup, may be incorrect. But what if you substitute the phrase "violent events" for "events"? What if violence itself is the syrup of our time, a syrup that we are not actually interested in but still need?

Gertrude Stein went on to praise herself, James Joyce, and Proust for writing fiction in which "nothing much happens." "For our purposes," she says, "events have no importance."

This claim, that events have no importance, is interesting to me because of its remarkable and stubborn absurdity. To find

events unimportant is to imagine oneself shielded from the ter-
rors of history. During World War II, Gertrude Stein was not
always shielded—she was at times deeply frightened—and after
that war she was once again interested in events.

Mixed with her silliness, however, are ideas and statements,
that, once heard, do not go away. "And so what I am trying to
make you understand," she wrote, "is that every contemporary writer has to find out what is the inner time-sense of his
contemporariness."

"The inner time-sense of his contemporariness"—what is this?
And what if the inner time-sense of our era has something to
do with stillness, stillness through which action flows, stillness
that has a quality of excitement to it, stillness that has not been
dulled by narcosis and information sickness? To answer this
question, we might begin with a novel from 1884—a novel satu-
rated with American violence.

> Two or three days and nights went by; I reckon I might say
> they swum by, they slid along so quiet and smooth and lovely.
> Here is the way we put in the time . . . we slid into the river and
> had a swim, so as to freshen up and cool off; then we set down
> on the sandy bottom where the water was about knee deep,
> and watched the daylight come. Not a sound, anywheres—
> perfectly still—just like the whole world was asleep, only some-
> times the bull-frogs a-cluttering, maybe.

Huck Finn follows this observation with a nineteen-line sentence, a sentence of over three hundred words that I won't quote
here but which is worth looking up, something of a rhapsody,
the longest sentence in his book, and, I think, one of the most
beautiful sentences in American literature. Near the beginning
of chapter nineteen of *Adventures of Huckleberry Finn*, the sen-

tence is therefore in close proximity to the death, by gunshot, of Huck's friend Buck Grangerford in chapter eighteen, and the death, also by gunshot, of Boggs, by Colonel Sherburn, in chapter twenty-one.

It is as if Americans typically have their moments of stillness when those moments are framed on both sides by violence. It is a peculiarly American form of Zen enlightenment, when stillness can only justify itself by planting itself amid uproar.

Stillness in fiction arises when the dramatic action pauses, and when the forward movement of thought appears to cease as well. Instead of the forward dramatic line we (at least temporarily) have the absorption of the character into the minutiae of the setting. The dynamics of desire and fear are momentarily displaced by a rapt attention to small details, to the cultivation of a moment's mood for its own sake without any nervous straining after insight. Stillness is not the same as an epiphany. Attention flows away from what is supposed to command it toward the peripheries: the river, the bank, the trash floating down the river, the sound of the cricket. In a moment of stillness, the atmosphere supplants the action.

In these moments, the setting may take on the burden of the feeling.

Any such moment is fascinating because, in most Western literature, it simply cannot last. Threatened by desire, cravings, and appetites of every variety, and by the onset of boredom, it has a kind of otherworldliness. For this reason, stillness has its sinister side: one of Burroughs's junkies staring for hours at his Florsheim shoe; or Andy Warhol's impenetrable presentation of a self-contained blank-faced narcissism; or Norman Bates, at the conclusion of *Psycho,* wrapped in his blanket, sitting immobilized in a room as blank as he is.

We might say about these forms of stillness that they have been traumatically fixated, unable to enlarge themselves or to develop. One's freedom in such instances, contaminated by an overpowering fear of shame or death, is the freedom not to make a move, *any* move. One becomes a junkie, or an artist, or a murderer, in order to enlarge one's capacities not to move, or to be moved.

In contemporary gothic mainstream literature, stillness at times has been shunted, or wrenched, away from pleasure and quietism, toward something that imitates the postures of death in an effort to fool it and to keep it safely at a distance. If you play dead, in these works, you won't die. One feels the presence of this kind of traumatized camouflage in several of Burroughs's novels, but also in the works of Kathy Acker, Bret Easton Ellis, Mary Gaitskill, and, in Europe, Botho Strauss and Ian McEwan. The landscape of contemporary fiction is full of this kind of camouflage, a sort of zombie dandyism.

My own interest in stillness has more to do with its benign features and with the great difficulty we have in expressing them. Because stillness lies toward the extremes of both the pleasure principle and the death instinct, it is often associated—perhaps unfortunately—with drugged blankness or morbidity. Boredom or deathliness keep trying to appropriate it. Imagine a person who stays on the phone with a lover, in a state of silent mutual happiness.To a third party this silence would probably give the wrong impression—that is, silence and stillness are always open to misinterpretation. From a distance ecstasy often looks a bit overdetermined.

"Be still," we say, usually to children. Learn to be quiet and settled. Or we say, "It's still here." It has survived something. In both these usages, the word is associated with peaceful endurance or calm. The state of calm can be dynamic. Charles Ives claimed that his music was meant to expose "a kind of furious calm."

I am having coffee with a friend. I tell her I am writing about stillness and ask her what books come to mind when I mention the subject. Virginia Woolf, she says, in *The Waves,* and Michael Ondaatje's writing generally, but *The English Patient* in particular. I myself have thought of Woolf, the dying away of the wind in the last section of *To the Lighthouse.* Or Proust: the opening pages of *Swann's Way* and the closing pages of *Time Regained.*

Another friend nods when I mention stillness. "Oh, right," he says. "The sections between the murders in *Pulp Fiction.* People sitting around and talking about nothing much, before they start shooting." Without meaning to, I agree with him. I forget to ask him if he means shooting a gun, or shooting up. It is not the shootings and murders in *Pulp Fiction* that interest people, but the sections in between, the sections full of talk. Nevertheless, the violence is necessary in order to make the stillness possible, as in *Huck Finn.* Violence frames it. For this reason, Tarantino's movie feels, much of the time, like a comedy or something with a joke structure. It is one instance of Gertrude Stein's claims about events: No one is interested in the violence in *Pulp Fiction,* but it is needed, like a narcotic fix, so that the rest of the story may go on.

Benign stillness is simply one of the hardest psychic conditions to get on paper, and when the effort fails, as it usually does, the result looks like bad prose poetry or aggressively oversensitive rhetoric. One has to struggle against the narrative necessities of fiction in order to get a moment of stillness into the story in the first place, and in this struggle, the tendency is to lurch toward overstatement, out of a fear of boring the reader. But there is boredom and *boredom*. The composer Erik Satie claimed that boredom was "mysterious and profound." All the same, few literary tonalities sound worse than an overstated and over-described hush, full of insufferable displays of bejeweled feelings.

It's just possible that benign stillness has become a condition in our time that everyone feels now and then but which almost no one can describe with much accuracy. This has everything to do with what adult readers will believe and accept about their own past experiences. My sense of these matters is that we have become remarkably fluent in our narratives in describing violence and complaint but timid and insecure in describing moments of repose. In the nineteenth century, the reverse was true. Chekhov, for example, writes absolutely convincing scenes of stasis, but he rushes through moments of violence, such as the child-murder scene in his story "In the Ravine," as if such violence were quite unbelievable.

The power of stillness: an intensifier, a marker, an ability to define what surrounds it, using antidramatic, antinarrative means. What all stories want to get to, but cannot for the most part include.

But the issue is even more basic than that, more personal. I like to imagine that stillness can be made worthy of our attention. If stillness can be given different shadings—erotic, sorrowful, even terse or endangered—then there is cause for hope in several directions at once. Think of how Chekhov, or for that matter Satie, made the condition of boredom endlessly dynamic.

If, however, we have truly lost the ability to be interested in stillness, in the intricacies of psychic motionlessness, then we will have lost the capacity to be accurate about an entire dimension of our experiences.

Three examples.

The Great Gatsby is so much a part of our national mythology and our required reading lists that its writerly oddities tend to be overlooked in the rush to get the book "prepared," and term papers written. In this novel and in *Tender Is the Night*, Fitzgerald regularly stops his scenes with a peculiar brilliance that's easy to miss. In *Gatsby* these tricks of timing are a sign of the narrator's, Nick Carraway's, habit of removing his perceptions from the scene in which he is participating, partly because he is dazzled, and partly because he is also suspicious of bedazzlement and emotional fraud. At times the stillness effect seems intended to evoke romantic longing. In all cases it sparks a characteristic feeling of odd wonder, a poisonously pleasant emotion in the presence of the wealth that the book is at pains to diagnose and to treat.

The first chapter is thick with such moments. Nick has arrived at the Buchanans. "The windows were ajar and gleaming white against the fresh grass outside that seemed to grow a little way into the house." This is a very odd sentence. It's surprising that it got past the Scribner copyeditors. Infused with the kind of bland surrealism you feel when you stare for too long at a Hopper painting, this moment is immediately followed by the famous paragraph in which Jordan and Daisy are introduced, seemingly airborne, both of them sitting on a sofa. As dazzling as they are, Nick is fixed on the peripheries. "I must have stood," he writes, "for a few moments listening to the whip and snap of the curtains and the groan of a picture on the wall."

Those few moments count for everything in this scene. They

comprise a piece of time in which Nick's consciousness has almost stopped. As a narrator, Nick will not be rushed. The whip
and the groan tell us that this is a haunted house, that the objects in it are complaining and halfway sentient, and they warn
us, in a sort of elegant comic gothic style, that all is not well at
the Buchanans. In the following sentence, Tom shuts the door
and "the caught wind died out about the room, and the curtain
and the rugs and the two young women ballooned slowly to the
floor." Notice how Tom has the ability to catch the wind and to
kill it. Notice how, in this moment of stillness, Tom pulls the
women earthward, how they descend to his level.

Fitzgerald was seldom afraid of literalizing his metaphors.
This gives his writing its characteristic cavalier glossiness and,
as he moved toward the composition of *Tender Is the Night,* its
progressive structural waywardness. In *Gatsby,* rugs and beautiful women could balloon to the floor because he believed, with
a touching faithfulness, that most readers could share his vision
and understand the figures for it. In his fiction there's a kind of
manic exhilaration in encountering beautiful objects, an exhilaration habitually deflated by a single brutal gesture. The punc-
turing of these balloons, the way things drift earthward, the
brutality behind the glare of riches—all these shattered displays
give *Gatsby* a curious rhythm. Stillness—a rapt gaze—alternates
with violence, very much in the American style. When I close
my eyes and imagine the book, I see its characters either standing immobilized, watching and waiting, or engaged in orgies or
automotive manslaughter or homicide. I cannot see anything
between these two poles.

Second example.

In chapter eight of Marilynne Robinson's *Housekeeping,*
Sylvie takes Ruth, her niece, to her "secret place," up the lake

from Fingerbone, to a site of abandoned homesteads. Sylvie has promised Ruth that children, or the spirits of children—she is characteristically vague on this point—may meet them there. But when they arrive on the spot, Sylvie abandons Ruth. Ruth goes into the cellar of a ruined, collapsed house, the remnant of a homestead, where she pulls out loose planks until she is sweating. She realizes that there are no spirit children there: "They were light and spare and thoroughly used to the cold, and it was almost a joke to them to be cast out into the woods, even if their eyes were gone and their feet were broken." Having thought this, Ruth sits down and waits for Sylvie to return.

The following passage is immune to quotation. It cannot be successfully excerpted. Its mixture of grieving and rapture seems to me to avoid the florid baroque in which some writers might have indulged. Marilynne Robinson, and Ruth, her narrator, quite possibly find stillness more interesting than action, with the result that the rhetoric does not need to be cranked up. In any case, in this section, Ruth is letting stillness inhabit her, allowing the chill to take her over, the literal chill and the metaphysical chill of Sylvie's abandonment of her. It's a moment of vision, and it is rapturous. Once Ruth has absorbed the cold, and absorbed the fact that the spirits will not return to her, Sylvie comes back, wraps Ruth in her overcoat, and rocks her. Then she takes her home across the water.

This section, like much of *Housekeeping*, feels deeply ritualistic to me. In it, gloom and wonder start to shift positions; Ruth's condition as a child, and Sylvie's status as an adult, never clear anywhere in the novel, are collapsed and pulled apart again. This section of the book seems to be fixated on the ground under Ruth, but the book insists that the ground on which one stands is a material illusion anyway, as is the first fundamental of that illusion, the house one lives in. Like Jay Gatsby, Sylvie seems to fall rather frequently into trance states. At first Ruth tries to pry her out of these states. Then she stops trying, and *Housekeeping* itself falls into the trance, into a condition of a prolonged and permanent hush.

Trances, spirits, stillness. It is tempting to say that these elements begin to come together in a condition of loss, that what we have been talking about all along is loss, that stillness and silence are collaborators in waiting, but waiting without knowing what we are waiting for, waiting without an object in view. This is one of the ways in which I understand the process of grieving. The ground underneath us becomes immaterial, and we wait in full knowledge that what we wait for will not appear. There can be a curious calm and alertness, an animal sensitivity, to this condition.

Elsewhere, in an essay on the American West, Marilynne Robinson has argued that our mythologies about the West are warped in the direction of gunplay, warfare and conquest, John Wayne, open spaces, and slaughter. What if, she suggests, alongside that noisy male-dominated set of myths, there is another one more commonly perceived by women, a West dominated by space and silence? A West of silences, in which the openness is an invitation not to action, but to what I have been calling here a trance condition?

Perhaps all along I have been talking about the Midwest, my home territory, and my persistent amazement about it.

Third and last set of examples: Wright Morris, *The Works of Love*, an American novel from 1952, and *Fire Sermon*, from 1971.

The Works of Love, about a man whose life never amounts to very much and who lives his life in a semitrance, is written in a relentlessly peculiar style. Things and people suddenly appear and vanish in it. Whole paragraphs are given over to digressions. After a few awkward gestures toward plot, the novel's story line, such as it is, renounces conflict in favor of meditation. Declarative sentences often switch direction and conclude with question marks. Even the efforts at characterization are halfhearted: The women in the novel are only half seen, if that, and often at a disadvantage. Transitions are abrupt, occasionally baffling. Isolated moments are elongated for pages, while years flash by like a deck of cards shuffled by an impatient dealer. If it were not for its seemingly banal Midwestern settings and lower-middle-class characters and laconic narrative voice, the book would have been classified long ago as European experimentalism at its most willful and extreme.

And yet the book has a subject, a clear one, and a clear means of addressing it. *The Works of Love* is about a man who wants to love but who in his bewilderment does not know how to go about it. Some element, common to others, is missing in his character. In most respects he is bewildered and stays that way all his life. In virtually all matters, he does not have a clue. Wright Morris has no interest in turning this situation into one that is meant to charm and seduce, à la *Forrest Gump*. His protagonist, Will Brady, draws a blank no matter where he is. He is not especially lovable, and the narrative keeps him at a distance. The result is a terribly eerie novel about a specific kind of American emptiness, an emptiness filled with things and pragmatism and people. Will Brady lives in a state of constant distraction. Having grown up on the great plains, he is infected with emptiness and takes it with him everywhere. "This desolate place [Morris writes], this rim of the world, had been God's country to Adam Brady, but to Caroline Clayton, a godforsaken hole. Perhaps only Will Brady could combine these two points of view. He could leave it, that is, but he could never get over it."

Which is to say that emptiness and the sacred are combined for him. If *Gatsby* has sentences of stillness, and *Housekeeping* long passages of it, then *The Works of Love* is an experiment of sorts in writing a novel with a central character who is still all the way through.

The lyrical emptiness of Will Brady's circumstances is conveyed, not in the European style through lavish attention to the vacancy of thought rising through higher and higher forms of abstraction, but through a careful attention to hotel lobbies, city parks, and railroad stations. In America every emotion, even emptiness, is supported by American *things*; our pragmatism seems to insist on this. The novel—I am not the first to make this observation about Wright Morris's fiction—feels like a succession of photographs. The photographs are taken with detachment but are lovingly assembled. The effect, however, is to reduce to nothing the dynamics of the action and to increase to absolute proportions the attention to things at rest. The effect is transfixing, very rich, and deeply disturbing.

With its constant shift of perspectives combined with its subject, the novel starts to feel like Grant Wood's *American Gothic* as repainted by Braque, as a cubist collage. The reader feels a bit stunned, as Will Brady does, at sea in an ocean of detail. The eye cannot find the proper object of its desire anywhere. It does not even know *where* to look, in this abundance of persistent muted objects. Desire gets lost, in this bland Midwestern Zen, even on Will Brady's wedding day. Here, for example, is a paragraph in which he forgets to look at his wife during the ceremony (he is looking through a doorway instead and, as usual, is transfixed):

> They were married in Bruno, a Bohemian town in the rolling
> country just south of the Platte, four or five miles' drive from

where her father had a big farm. They were married in the church where Ralph Bassett had married her. It sat on the rise, overlooking the town, and as it was June the door stood open and Will Brady could see the buggies drawn up beneath the shade trees out in front. An elderly man was combing sandburs from a dark mare's tail. It was quiet on the rise, without a leaf stirring, but in the sunny hollow along the tracks a westerly breeze was turning the wheel of a giant windmill. It looked softly blurred, quite a bit the way the heat made everything look in Indian Bow, with the air, like a clear stream of water, flowing up from the hot earth. Near the windmill a man was sinking a post, and the sound of the blows, like jug corks popping, came up in the pause that his mallet hung in the air. Fred Blake had to remind him—nudging him sharply—to kiss the bride.

This is thickly lyrical but it would be a mistake to call it heartwarming. The narrative, taking Will Brady's side of things, collaborates with him by somehow not noticing his wife. She is dramatically at the center of this scene, but the drama has been pushed to the periphery, and the peripheries (the windmill, the mallet) have been nudged to the center, in the interest of stillness. I think Morris wants to convey a feeling of loneliness and distraction at the center of action here, but I don't think "alienation" is the right word for that feeling. It can hit any of us when we are not quite inside the action we are performing, and it is intensified, for example at parties or other social gatherings, when we are supposed to be feeling emotions that we may not have—when public displays of sentiment are called for—but acting seems out of the question.

Many readers, baffled or frustrated by the gruff, dry displacement of drama in Morris's fiction, may give up on it before the love for places and things becomes evident. Like the otherwise dissimilar Willa Cather and Jack Kerouac, Morris is often in an elegiac mode, writing about, to use one of his favorite phrases from Samuel Beckett, "things about to disappear." As a photographer, Morris has shown himself to be transfixed—that word again—by objects, both human and inanimate, that have sustained much use. They have been weathered, and in his photographs and his fiction they possess a gaunt, stark geometry.

The Works of Love details dispassionately Will Brady's failure as a chicken farmer (his hens die) and as a home builder (he neglects to install a furnace in his basement), and as a father and husband, but in a sense the novel has been waiting all along for Will Brady to get old, for his baffled heartiness to spin upon a still point—a park bench or a rented room. Late in the novel, living in a rooming house, Will Brady finds himself once again alone, and in the evenings he walks down toward Lincoln Park. This situation provokes the narrative into an extraordinary tight-lipped grandeur:

> If there was a moon, or a cool breeze off the lake, Will Brady would walk through the park to the water, where he would stroll along the pilings, or under the trees on the cinder bridle path. He had walked on cinders, he seemed to remember, somewhere before. As he had in the past, he would have to sit down and tap them out of his shoes. In the dusk there would be lights on in the Wrigley tower, an air-plane beacon would sweep the sky, and at Oak Street beach people would be lying in the warm sand. The drinking fountain would give off a strong chlorine smell. He would wet his face at the fountain, then take his seat among those people who had come to the beach but didn't care to take off their clothes; who had been hot in their rooms, and perhaps lonely in their minds. In the dark they could speak what they had on their minds without troubling about their faces, the sound of their voices, or

who their neighbor was. Will Brady was their neighbor. He sat with his coat folded in his lap, his shirtsleeves rolled.

That's beautiful. It goes on for another three pages. It moves somewhere between detachment, placidity, and the inevitability of sadness. Will Brady's story has been subsumed here into a Chicago nocturne. The story, such as it is, can wait.

In another one of his novels, *Fire Sermon,* Wright Morris follows a boy and his aged Uncle Floyd as they break into the house of Floyd's sister, empty of her, but still filled with her things.

The boy said, "Aren't there any lights?" and looked for the switch on the wall. There was no switch, but on the table at the bedside stood a lamp, with a green shade, a wick curled in the bowl of clear oil. Uncle Floyd kicked the door, opening it wider, then stomped in to throw up the blind at the window opening out on the porch. That did little good because it was blocked by the iceboxes. The room smelled of burned lamp wick, coal oil, and the odor the boy associated with his mother's clothes closet, at once sweet and sour. On the floor was a saucer of soured milk, the edges nibbled by mice. A shoebox full of postcard pictures of cats, kittens, and puppies, along with postcards and letters, sat on the shelf below the lamp. The boy recognized the last letter, with the Smokey the Bear stamp, as his own. On the table at the foot of the bed, where they could be reached through the iron frame, soiled towels and dishcloths were piled in a washbowl, held down by a plate dirty with food smears. At the side a comb is stuck into the bristles of a brush with a silver back, and a small oval picture in a frame stamped with colored flowers. The picture showed a bearded man, seated erect on a chair, with a child on his knee holding a bird cage. The boy moved closer to see if the cage held a bird, but it is empty and the door is open. A woman stands behind him, one white hand resting on his shoulder, her hair parted and gathered in a bun at the neck.

This rhapsodic inventory—the things Aunt Viola carried—is wonderfully unstable. It cannot stay in the past tense and shifts uneasily into the present. The woman in the photograph comes out of the photograph, and, through a trick of faulty reference, puts her hand on the boy's shoulder. The description of Aunt Viola's house goes on for several more pages, and eventually the inventory includes the boy's uncle.

> "Uncle Floyd," the boy said, but remained standing in the door. The green blind softened the light, and with nothing in the room to block it or absorb it the boy felt its presence. Within it, captive, he saw the figure seated on the narrow-backed armless rocker, both the seat and the back covered with pads made of patchwork quilting. Two dozen patches on the back side alone, in all shapes, colors, and materials. Everything left over had been put into it, as into this house. The old man who sat there did not impress the boy as his own great-uncle, Floyd Warner, but another object preserved from the past. Perhaps this corner room had been reserved for objects of that sort . . . The boy really knew nothing about such matters and perhaps that proved to his advantage. He brought so little to what he saw, he saw what was there.

This reminds me of Kerouac, but Kerouac after detox, and it is very close to the emotion of entranced waiting we find in *Housekeeping*. Speculation—in both senses of that word—is at work here. This kind of writing takes nerve and confidence to do, to assume that the reader will adapt to this vision and will be patient enough to wait for the next action, when it eventually comes. The style does not share Fitzgerald's Princetonian confidence that the metaphorical visions will be magically conveyed to the reader. It's too dour for that. Stillness has fully inhabited this narrative voice; like the prose writing of Samuel Beckett, a stoic lyric intelligence seems to be aware of the reader but eager to keep some distance from that reader. In order to create its atmosphere, the excitement of its contemporariness, it must slow down, rather than speed up, and turn its back slightly to us.

The purpose of this slowdown is to locate a sense of wonder squarely at the center of the story. Wright Morris's intelligence is such that he constantly withdraws from the scene of his own story in order to express his wonder at it, and, in a sense, his detachment from it. It takes nerve to keep the action moving, but it takes more nerve to slow it down or to stop it, and a particular kind of courage to keep what seems to be peripheral at the center. Morris's fiction—like Charles Reznikoff's and Lorine Niedecker's poetry—has this nerve and eccentricity as its trademark, mostly, I think at the service of wonder.

Morris is quite explicit about this. In the last chapter of *Fire Sermon* the boy finds a coin "in the pocket of a coat, draped on a doornail, that had survived all the people who had spent or saved it since 1879. The meaning of this escaped him in a manner he found satisfying. Already he was old enough to gaze in wonder at life." Wonderment never quite gets used to whatever it is looking at.

So finally we arrive at wonder, which, for me, is at the bottom level, the ground floor, of stillness. Wonder is at the opposite pole of worldliness, just as stillness is at the opposite pole from worldly action. Wonder puts aside the known and accepted, along with sophistication, and instead serves up an intelligent naïveté. Why should anything be as it is? Why are things as they are? What if some fiction thrives, not on statements and claims, but on questions? Wonder is about the last emotion one would expect to find in contemporary America, and that gives it a power to dramatize the excitement of contemporariness, with meanings that will escape us in a manner we will all find satisfying.

Notes

Walter Benjamin, "The Storyteller," in *Illuminations*. Edited by Hannah Arendt, translated by Harry Zohn (New York: Schocken Books, 1969): 83–110.

Gertrude Stein, "How Writing Is Written," in *How Writing Is Written*. Edited by Robert Bartlett Haas (Los Angeles: Black Sparrow Press, 1974): 151–160.

Regarding Happiness

1. *Staying on in the Garden*

After a small press published my first book of poetry in 1970, I happened to be visiting my parents for a few days. On one particular evening late in my visit, my mother sat down with me during the cocktail hour, a time when she often appeared to be emboldened. She held my book in her hand. Her martini was nearby, within easy reach. She studied me with a frozen smile and altered her position slightly on the sofa to give the impression that she felt relaxed; this impression failed.

"I've read your book," my mother said. "I was very impressed." The frozen smile did not fade.

"Thank you." I nodded.

"I just have this one question," she said, digging for a cigarette in a mostly empty pack, having put down the book by now on the sofa cushion. She lit the cigarette, taking her time; she was in no hurry. She inhaled, and as she asked her question, smoke blew out of her nose and mouth. "My question is, when are you going to write a happy poem?"

Thirty-seven years later, I cannot remember what I replied,

but I hope I didn't say what probably occurred to me: "Well, okay, when I'm happy, *then* I'll write a happy poem."

Questions like the one my mother posed seem innocent, even comical, but after all, she *was* my parent and was probably dismayed by my poetry and by the thoughts, images, and feelings displayed within it. Good! I wanted my poetry to dismay everybody. That was its purpose.

Anyone who has taught literature probably has had a similar moment, when the students in class complain that the texts they have been assigned to study are "depressing." The stories are "morbid." Their endings are "sad." Sometimes the students become more aggressive in the pursuit of good cheer. "Why," they ask, "can't we read some novels and stories about happiness?"

Such questions seem inevitable: After all, eighteen- and nineteen-year-olds are the understudies for adulthood and would like to clutch at innocence for as long as they can. Besides, what they're asking for goes to the heart of what literature can and (often) cannot do. When I myself was a freshman at Macalester College, our teacher, a hipster classicist and translator of Pindar, answered our particular version of this question (we had been reading *The Oresteia*) by saying, "Fine. We can read stories about happiness if you want to. Where are they? *What* are they?"

We met his questions with our baffled silence. Then a brave soul mentioned Dante's *Paradiso*. "But that isn't happiness," our teacher said. "That's joy. That's religious exaltation." He waited. "Can anyone name a serious twentieth-century novel with a happy ending?" More silence. "I thought so," he said.

The political force of happy endings become additionally complicated by the power of the state. If you can imagine Joseph Stalin asking Osip Mandelstam why he was not writing cheerful poetry, or inquiring of Dimitry Shostakovich on the front page of *Pravda* when he would stop writing muddles instead of music, the question about happiness-in-art no longer seems particularly harmless. In the Soviet Union this particular inquisition constituted a matter of life and death to its citizens. Our eloquent unhappiness seems to make those who are in power very uneasy. But their uneasiness is merely one of several problems in addressing the depiction of happiness in literature. The question might better be framed: Where, and how, *is* happiness depicted? And why is it nearly impossible to portray it in extended dramatic narratives? In this way, a small problem turns into one that seems almost unimaginably vast: *What is the matter with happiness?*

That great wit Oscar Levant, from the depths of his drug addiction, insomnia, broken nervous system, and wrecked career in music and the movies, once said, "Happiness isn't something you experience; it's something you remember."

Some epigrams just seem clever. This one has a sadly detached nagging truth to it, proceeding from a knowingness about the strange blank emptiness of those happy blessed isles somewhere off in the distance where you can't get at them. *Happiness, we might say, usually has no consciousness of itself.* When happiness occurs, it rarely reflects back on its own condition—after all, why should it? As an emotion complete in its own magical circle, happiness requires nothing beyond what it already has. Longing, for example, yearns for an object that happiness has already found. Contentment certainly does not need more thoughts or speculations that might, in fact, endanger it. In this sense, happiness is typically blind to its own situation.

We all understand intuitively that reading about the happiness of others is often boring. Adam and Eve in the Garden do nothing in particular; they are virtually non-narratable. Adam does not sit down and engage in troubled speculation concerning why he feels so good all day long. He has no compulsion to question his condition; no one, including God, is requiring him to think, or, for that matter, requiring him to do anything. Adam has no stories to tell, either. He says, "Another perfect day in Paradise." (He does not, however, understand what the word "perfect" means, since everything is perfect; the word therefore has no meaning for him. Nor does "Paradise.") Adam does not say, "This day was better than other days," because that would imply that there had been a few bad days, and Adam has never had a bad day. To Eve, he says, "I love you." Unfortunately or not, he does not understand what love is, or what its opposite might be. The word we have for Adam's condition, therefore, is "innocence."

The Greek philosophers, those enemies of innocence, rarely discuss happiness and instead devote their attention to the good, or to the relation between pleasure and justice or virtue. Aristotle, near the beginning of the *Ethics,* simply argues that ". . . happiness is an activity of the soul in conformity with virtue, an activity of a certain kind." The happy man contemplates the good; circumstances do not alter him; he takes the middle way. In Greek tragedy, by contrast, the chorus, sticking to generalities, says that the greatest good fortune is simply never to have been born at all. A few thousand years later, Karl Marx argues that global unhappiness will end altogether when the laborer is no longer alienated from the products of his work. Montaigne, who often worried about unhappiness, claims that we cannot know whether a person's life has been happy until we watch him die, at which point we will recognize whether he has been a hypocrite or not, an idea borne out later in Tolstoy's "The Death of Ivan Ilych."

To argue about happiness in the abstract, though difficult,

may be easier than to depict it dramatically in an interesting way, as fiction writers learn to their consternation. Most people have their own theories of happiness, which are not clichés, exactly, but conventions: The picture may include shelter, a relationship, a family, some meaningful work, freedom from hunger, a sufficiency of money. Having said that, are we then to write about the happy woman in her house, her happy babies, her happy husband? Or the happy lesbian? Or the happy transgendered account executive? And then what? What's interesting about them and their stories in the long run? Their happiness may be the least interesting thing about them. The Germans have a phrase, *das Glück im Winkel,* happiness in a corner, referring to a particular species of happiness that arises from a contentment with the things you have, i.e., a state of being free from the longing for things that you don't own. As it is described in Jonathan Strong's story "Tike," such happiness is made up of the "small things, your library, your hearth, a good meal, family and close friends, some music, a dog, modest sorts of things." None of this seems particularly interesting or rewarding as fictional material, however.

We all feel (again, intuitively) that there is something deeply uninteresting, perhaps banal, in the depiction—perhaps even the life—of a happy individual. Narratives designed to hold our interest seem to depend on trouble, conflict, secrets, duplicity, pain, cheating, lying, violence, sexual activities of every splendidly grungy variety and kind—all the features of an adult life. The very sight of happiness may offend those who see it. But why?

We need to turn back to the twin problems of *innocence* and *blindness.* For the sake of argument, let's suppose that to be happy a person must momentarily forget, or not see, the misfortunes of others. Further: What if our happiness *depends* on the unhappiness of others? What if the unhappiness of others

is a necessary condition to our own happiness? How can we ignore the suffering of everybody else? Frank Bidart's poem "The
War of Vaslav Nijinsky" gets at this problem very succinctly:

He learned that

All life exists

at the expense of other life . . .

The rich man manages to be rich only because there are many
poor men who have been forced to contribute to his wealth. The
well-fed man has dined on a lamb, or a calf, or a cauliflower. *All
life exists,* Bidart/Nijinsky says, *at the expense of other life.* The
wolf in its animal-unknowingness may not be troubled by the
vole's sacrifice to the wolf's appetite, but a person whose eyes
have been opened notices the nature of all sacrifice; he can't help
but notice.

As William S. Burroughs said, "A paranoid-schizophrenic is
a guy who just found out what's going on."

The innocent soul who has somehow never learned this particular lesson leaves the movie theater saying, "I didn't like it. It
was depressing." The innocent soul finishes the story and says, "It
was sad. It was disheartening. Let's go drink beer and play video
games." The story and the movie have somehow *not come home*
to this person; their stories don't seem profound, just gloomy.
But close-mindedness of this sort, when forcibly extended in
time and space, may seem criminally innocent, even insane. An
upbeat president of the United States may be dangerously opti-
mistic as long as he remains profoundly incurious about what
he doesn't know and doesn't want to find out about; meanwhile,
he sets soldiers and Marines out on a badly defined task. He
walks about in a cloud of highly calculated ignorance, his fire-

power protected by his impermeable unawareness. Incuriosity is one of the first warning signs of willed innocence, enforced innocence, and a childish incorruptibility for which Americans are known and feared throughout the globe.

To complain about a tragic work of art is to be afraid or resentful of the pain of others. Such a reaction removes the observer from a position of sympathy to one of resistance. But suppose you are not blind and have never been either blind or innocent; suppose you have seen some of the worst events of the twentieth century. How, then, might you write a poem about happiness? Here is Czeslaw Milosz's poem "Gift." Milosz translated the poem from the original Polish.

> A day so happy.
> Fog lifted early, I worked in the garden.
> Hummingbirds were stopping over honeysuckle flowers.
> There was no thing on earth I wanted to possess.
> I knew no one worth my envying him.
> Whatever evil I had suffered, I forgot.
> To think that once I was the same man did not embarrass me.
> In my body I felt no pain.
> When straightening up, I saw the blue sea and sails.

When I recited this poem to a friend, also a poet, he said, "It sounds Chinese." What is particularly interesting about "Gift" is that its rhetorical gestures in the direction of happiness consist almost entirely of negations. Note that there is only a minimal narrative thread. The speaker is not greedy (line four), not envious (line five), not vindictive or melancholy (line six), not shameful (line seven), not in pain (line eight). The poem traces out a *via negativa,* a happiness made possible by various absences and blanks. Each negation seems to constitute a kind of triumph and is signaled by the period at the end of each

line. This is true. Stop. That is true. Stop. By Aristotle's definition, the speaker is virtuous, free from cravings and anguish,
and he works in a pastoral setting, a garden, the site of paradise.
Happiness is thus not just a state of being but a state of being
discovered in the midst of an activity.

But "Gift" is not the product of an innocent mind; there had
been no fault of human character unknown to Czeslaw Milosz.
We must note that the poet cannot formulate happiness without evoking the world of envy, greed, pain, shame, and suffering
that happiness does not, at this moment, inhabit; happiness here
exists within a dialectic and is defined in terms of what it disowns; furthermore, this condition seems momentary and evanescent. Milosz, like William Wordsworth, here seems surprised
by joy. Happiness in the garden is transitory. The poem assumes
that night will follow the day. A child might see the garden,
the hummingbird, and the blue sky and sails, and only those
things, within that narrow field; but the adult sees everything
else, the envy and the greed, etc. Also the hourglass. Somehow,
Milosz manages to hold on to the doubleness of consciousness
without losing his sense of felicity or good fortune. A minor
miracle, and he knows it.

Point number 1: *A mindful happiness knows, and acknowledges, everything from which it has been excluded or freed. It
often has a frame of suffering around it.*

Point number 2: *Happiness, within a dramatic medium, requires an activity to serve as its vehicle.*

At the end of Ernest Hemingway's *In Our Time* the reader
finds a story in two parts, "Big Two-Hearted River," nominally
about fishing. But the story follows narratives set in and around
World War I, stories about betrayals, suffering, violence, and
suicide; and "Big Two-Hearted River" itself is divided down the
middle, as many commentators have noticed, by a vignette con-

cerning a terrified man, Sam Cardinella, condemned to death by hanging, who loses control of his bowels on his way to the gallows.

Death surrounds "Big Two-Hearted River." But inside the story Nick Adams tramps his way to a river, where he fishes for trout and for eleven pages is guardedly happy and then blissful. The story constitutes itself as a kind of instruction manual. 1. *Take your time.* "He did not want to rush his sensations any." 2. *Don't bring along strangers.* "Unless they were of your party, they spoiled it." 3. *Don't be greedy.* "Nick had one good trout. He did not care about getting many trout." 4. *Don't feel guilty about trivial matters.* "He was settled. Nothing could touch him." 5. *Know how to go about doing what you like to do.* "Nick felt awkward and professionally happy with all his equipment hanging from him." 6. *Remember that the time for paradise is short; the hour will run out.* ". . . in the fast deep water, in the half light, the fishing would be tragic. In the swamp fishing was a tragic adventure."

Undergraduate readers, exposed to this story, tend to find it frustrating and unfocused and experimental. "There's no story." Or: "Where's the plot?" Or: "Nothing happens." To which my answer always has been: Didn't you ask for a story about happiness? Well, here it is. You said you wanted happiness, but when I present it to you, you find it dull and empty.

Most of the stories about happiness deal with an activity successfully completed; this is the narrative cover under which they typically do their work. Mrs. Ramsay's dinner party in Virginia Woolf's *To the Lighthouse* leads to a famous moment in which Mrs. Ramsay looks down at the table and feels that "there is a coherence in things, a stability; something, she meant, is immune from change, and shines out . . . so that again tonight she had the feeling she had had once today already, of peace, of rest." A similar happiness results when James steers the boat to the lighthouse at the novel's end. "Well done!" his father says, and James "was so pleased that he was not going to let anybody share a grain of his pleasure."

Mrs. Dalloway, in the novel named after her, is about to have a social gathering and needs to acquire flowers. Septimus Smith, wounded and mad, wanders off in the distance somewhere, but he does not destroy Mrs. Dalloway's happiness in her task. Albert Camus insists that we consider Sisyphus, in his futile chore of rolling the stone up the hill, as a happy man.

In Malcolm Lowry's story "The Forest Path to the Spring," happiness consists of getting water every day for the household from a neighboring creek. Note the pastoralism again. It seems as if we are constantly returning to a garden in this mode, a garden bordered by a darkening city. When we aren't, we're in the presence of an innocence that has never been corrupted by adulthood or power, that cannot see the attractions of either one and remains almost childishly unfallen; the garden, so to speak, remains stubbornly inside.

Point number 3: *A prolonged innocence, and the happiness that arises from it, is nearly always comic.*

Such is the condition of Mr. Pickwick in *Pickwick Papers*. In an essay on Pickwick, W. H. Auden makes the point:

> It is the story of a man who is innocent . . . and is, therefore, living in Eden. He then eats of the Tree . . . [and] becomes conscious of the reality of Evil but, instead of falling from innocence into sin . . . he changes from an innocent child into an innocent adult who no longer lives in an imaginary Eden of his own but in the real and fallen world ("Dingley Dell & The Fleet").

By this definition, Candide is almost happy, Bertie Wooster *is* happy, as are Chauncey Gardiner in Jerzy Kosinski's *Being*

There and Anton Chekhov's Olga Semyonovna in "The Darling." These types are traditional comic characters whose innocence serves as a contrast and disruption to the disillusioned world around them. There is a neat comic incongruity between the world's rank tragic slop and the weird contentment and adaptability of these characters, as if they could see everything surrounding them but somehow couldn't begin to process it inwardly the way everyone else does. As the novelist Christopher Bram has reminded me, happiness often arises from a character's adaptability to changing conditions.

In our time, no writer has pushed harder at such comic incongruity than the American writer Laurie Colwin. Colwin's characteristic story—her vision—is approximately as follows. All men are children and remain children until women force them to grow up. If a man doesn't find the right woman, he is unlikely ever to stop being a child. A woman causes a man to fall from his own innocence, not by teaching him anything (this would propel the story toward the world of Jane Austen's novels), but by provoking in him emotions of such seriousness and weight that he cannot go on being a child after having been struck by those feelings. This can also apply, in Colwin's fiction, to a gay man or woman who falls seriously in love and wants to enter a monogamous same-sex relationship. Love, in Colwin, wakes up a man to the world of adult gravity. For this reason, bachelors are often the only inhabitants of Eden; they remain weightless. Something about them resists becoming fully human; the helium balloons of humanity, they float through life.

Colwin tended to be a relentless ironist. Her own *Family Happiness* is modeled on Tolstoy's "Family Happiness," but with jokes attached, and the example of Kitty and Levin in *Anna Karenina* as a happy couple seems to have nagged at her. Her novel *Happy All the Time* (1978) presents us with two couples, complete with two neat pairings-off. The only trouble presented within the book is embodied in a young malcontent, Misty Berkowitz, a woman who stirs her coffee with her fountain pen and who has a tragic outlook trapped within a comic narrative—men, she believes, are mostly absurd; happiness is an illusion; matrimony is a sham; love, if it exists, is a snare.

The novel's plot exists, of course, to refute these views and to arrive at a good marriage. Whether the book's resolution happens to be plausible depends upon the prejudices of the individual reader. Myself, I love the book but find its characters nearly insufferable and its plot rather silly.

2. *Regarding Happiness*

When I was about sixteen, I went to a nearby town one day in July to see an outdoor festival on a lake. This festival included swimming and canoe races. After one of the canoe races, the winner, a strong handsome guy, grabbed his blue ribbon and went over to where a girl was standing in front of me. He was wearing swim trunks and presented an impressive physical spectacle. She smiled with recognition and then kissed him. She was beautiful—long hair, great body, terrific smile. She was everything I wanted and never seemed to have. After she kissed this guy, they turned toward the lake, the two of them, and she took his muscled right arm and wrapped it around her own waist, a gesture of great intimacy and contentment.

Forty years later, and I still remember it. I remember exactly how I felt that day, watching those two. I would bet that they don't remember themselves and that moment anymore; but I do.

I'd argue that in 80 percent of all narratives, the young couple and their happiness are not the story; the story resides in the *unhappy onlooker*—Satan, watching Adam and Eve; Claggert, staring at Billy Budd; Iago, looking at Othello and Desdemona;

Strether, gazing at Chad Newsome and Mme. de Vionnet in their boat; Jack Burden, looking at Willie Stark; Laura, up on her balcony, observing the vulgar and happily love-sick Braggioni in "Flowering Judas." In our own time, my friend Jim Shepard has specialized, in his beautifully eloquent, dark and comic stories, in dramatizing the exclusion of young adults from the garden; again and again in his narratives, a misfit's innocence is trampled and destroyed. Delmore Schwartz describes this condition in his poetry. "They are in the real!" his poems cry out, quoting Kafka, referring to those damnable insufferable happy people as seen by those who are stuck outside the gates. In other words: "Beautiful world—for *you*," to cite a Kafkaesque rock band, Devo.

Which leads me to my final, central text: John Cheever's "The Worm in the Apple."

This is a very peculiar story. It is very short—three and a half pages. It gets up some momentum and then seemingly runs out of gas. The story concerns the Crutchmans, who "were so very, very happy and so temperate in all their habits and so pleased with everything that came their way that one was bound to suspect a worm in their rosy apple..." The story, in effect, looks for a story. It tries to discover some conflict, some trouble, some rot, or at least some decline—something in this family to serve as the foundation stone for a narrative, and, one assumes, as comfort for the rest of us. But the Crutchmans will not submit to the whole narrative business. They refuse its necessities. The Crutchmans are rich, religious, sexually active, white, heterosexual, apparently in love, well adjusted to their upper-class suburban lives. He's a lawyer, she's inherited money. They have two children, a boy and a girl. Both children grow up and marry well. Some dangers present themselves: Larry Crutchman has been in the war and survived four days in a lifeboat; Helen has inherited scads of money, but, it turns out, is not selfish or waste-ful. They are not traumatized, not ignorant, not unfaithful, not obnoxious. The children, Rachel and Tom, might have gone bad and married the wrong person, and the narrator, at one point, gleefully imagines a rough end for the daughter: "What, but chance, was there to keep her from ending up as a hostess at a Times Square dance hall?" But chance leads her to a good man, who takes a Ph.D. in physics and who becomes a teacher. For them, happily ever after!

The story becomes exasperated with itself. *Where is the story?* the story seems to ask, with more than a trace of irritation. Where is the worm in the apple? *It must be there somewhere.* After all, every story must contain its worm, as does every bottle of mescal. Stories begin when things start to go wrong. But, no: In the story's last paragraph, the narrator begins to wonder whether this exasperatingly happy couple presents a problem not for themselves but for him, the restless observer, who is re-garding their happiness with increasing irritation and, it seems, envy, and who is, not incidentally of course, a storyteller. The storyteller is apparently blameworthy, or so he claims: "through timidity or moral cowardice, [he] could not embrace the broad range of their natural enthusiasms and would not grant that, while Larry played neither Bach nor football very well, his plea-sure in both was genuine."

Why can't the narrator grant Larry his genuine pleasures? What happens if he *does* grant the Crutchmans their happiness? Well, to state the obvious: If he grants them their happiness, he has no story, and if he has no story, he has no reason for being there; it's a form of narrative suicide. Also: If the Crutchmans are so lucky to have an apple without a worm, what have they done to deserve their good fortune? Anything at all? Why don't the rest of us get that apple without that worm? The Crutchmans, it seems, are slightly unreal. They are exceptional. And, in a related sense, they are repulsive.

The story ends in what might be described as excited rage:

> The touchstone of their euphoria remained potent, and while Larry gave up the fire truck he could still be seen at the communion rail, the fifty-yard line, the 8:03, and the Chamber Music Club, and through the prudence and shrewdness of Helen's broker they got richer and richer and richer and lived happily, happily, happily, happily.

An adverb that has to be repeated four times is an adverb that somehow hasn't done its job and lacks credibility. It is a suspicious adverb. It constitutes a stutter. The end? *Happily ever after,* indeed, for these two? But perhaps the story has not been about the Crutchmans at all; perhaps, as the narrator observes at the last minute, as he withdraws from the awful scene of bliss that he himself has created, the story has been about the narrative stance of the narrator, something of a worm himself, or a serpent, looking for a subject of interest into which he might crawl. His consciousness is dominated by the unhappiness that binds him to others and to all stories about a world of misfits and of conflicts that arise from discontent and fugitive desire and need, which he does not find among any of the Crutchmans. Not finding it, the worm without a rot to chew on and digest, the narrative voice becomes momentarily hysterical. A certain mania takes over, a crazed expressive exclusion characteristic of the damned. "Happily, happily, happily, happily." Any reader is free to hear any tone she wants to hear in this line, but if the line means what it says, the story has, in effect, run off the tracks.

Something is wrong, of course, and what is wrong is that the Crutchmans don't belong to the world of literature. They are immune to it, or at least immune to its narrative compulsions.

Like Adam before the Fall, the Crutchmans are non-narratable, at least in the mode that Cheever has chosen (some other mode might permit a narration for them, but not this one), and in this mode they escape the storyteller's net he keeps trying to fling over them. Their happiness renders them insubstantial and empty—impertinent. They may be happy, but they are narratively sterile. They don't need us, and we return the favor: We don't care about them.

As a storyteller, the narrator requires the Crutchmans' unhappiness and discontent and failure and mania, but they won't give him what he needs. They refuse to shoulder his particular burden as he attempts to ascend the incline of the Freitag triangle. Therefore: the narrator, to provide balance, takes on the unhappiness and discontent and failure and mania that his characters refuse to take on; we are placed, finally, in the story's last lines, not with the Crutchmans, who live in the garden and who don't notice us—they are not, of course, readers of their own story or maybe of ours, either—but with the narrator, whom we might as well call "John Cheever."

At every crucial narrative turn, John Cheever's fictional strategies and dramatic constructions were characterized by restlessness. And restlessness, that friend to drama, possibly serves as *the* core enemy of happiness. All mankind's troubles, says Blaise Pascal, arise from our inability to sit still in a room. The anonymous Chinese poet of the Da zhao, "The Great Summons," after warning the soul not to go to the north, south, east, or west, commands, "O soul, come back to leisure and quietness! / Enjoy yourself in your land of Chu, tranquil and untroubled."

Or, in the words of Bob Dylan, in "Time Passes Slowly":

Ain't no reason to go in a wagon to town,
Ain't no reason to go to the fair.

Ain't no reason to go up, ain't no reason to go down,
Ain't no reason to go anywhere.

This has always sounded to me like the contentment of happiness, or of its second cousin once-removed, depression.

But perhaps Harold Pinter should be given the last word on this subject, the subject of happiness in a dramatic medium. In a recent profile in the *New York Times,* he said, "How can you write a happy play? . . . Drama is about conflict and general degrees of perturbation, disarray. I've never been able to write a happy play, but I've been able to enjoy a happy life."
Good for him.

for Karen and Jim Shepard

Note

Sonya's Last Speech, or, Double-Voicing: An Essay in Sixteen Sections

1. *My Chekhov Problem*

The Fifth Forum movie theater in Ann Arbor, before it became the Ann Arbor Theater and then was closed (now it's a seedy singles' bar called "Closer" or "Closer"—I don't know which way to pronounce it), was, in its day, one of those low-tech operations that existed before the advent of multiplexes. One employee would sell tickets, another would dole out the popcorn and candy, and a third sat up in the projection booth, dozing between reels. In the early 1980s it was one of the only theaters in southeastern Michigan where you could go to see independent and foreign films. I went there often, usually by myself. I'd buy my popcorn and sit down in the back because I don't like to sit close; I get headaches. In theaters like the Fifth Forum, your shoes would often slip on the greasy floor because of random deposits of buttered popcorn, and in fact the smell of candy wrappers and grease now has the association for me of what I'd call movie-longing, the sugared buttery smell of someone else's desires coming to life on the screen.

The Fifth Forum is the only theater where I've walked out

on the same movie twice. The movie in question was *My Dinner with Andre,* with Wallace Shawn and Andre Gregory. The first time I saw it, I thought it was a pretentious piece of downtown pseudo-art—a kitschy talkfest for intellectuals—and I walked out after about thirty-five minutes. I thought the script was insubstantial and found Andre Gregory insufferable. But then I read the reviews and was almost shouted at by my highbrow friend for having turned my back on this monument to the cinematic art, so I paid my admission again a week later and sat down and watched about forty minutes of it before walking out again into the late-spring Ann Arbor night.

A few years later, a movie called *Vanya on 42nd Street* came to the Fifth Forum, and I thought: *I'd better go see this, even if I don't want to.* For one thing, it had the dire combination of Wallace Shawn and Andre Gregory again, though this time with Shawn as actor and Gregory as director, in an adaptation of Anton Chekhov's *Uncle Vanya,* a play I knew pretty well. Duty sent me down there. I could imagine some academic Grand Inquisitor at a cocktail party asking me ("you're a literary type, right?") whether I had seen it and my flustered response that, no, last weekend I had gone to see *Aliens.*

The truth is that I always have had a Chekhov problem. It's serious. My Chekhov problem is that I usually go through a siege of boredom with his plays and stories before I arrive at a condition of aesthetic excitement. With me, it's either boredom or excitement, nothing in between. In a way, I am like a Chekhov character, who sits passively for three acts before getting his gun in the last act. In the stories, there is a large element of gray—even in Russian, according to Nabokov, the prose feels gray—and sometimes, in my late-twentieth-/early-twenty-first-century way, I'm just not up for the path through the monochrome to the small, perfectly placed explosions. This is my failing, and I hate these moments because they expose me to myself as the philistine that I know myself to be, especially after work, when I want to see cars explode and people shot dead for no reason, and monsters, if they're available, to cheer me up.

So anyway I sat there in the Fifth Forum, my shoes slipping on the popcorn butter on the floor and a recalcitrant spring in the seat giving my ass a poke every now and then. The movie came on, with its rehearsal framework, and I thought: *There's Larry Pine playing Dr. Astrov, he's pretty good.* And then—it had been a long day of teaching in Detroit at Wayne State—I felt myself drifting off to yawn-and-sleepy time, but through sheer willpower, and aided by my Coca-Cola, I managed to stay awake in a state of half-dozing twilight consciousness, waiting for the first speech in the play that I care about, Sonya's outburst about how plain she is. Sonya, in this production, was played by Brooke Smith, an actor (in those days we said "actress") I had never heard of.

Brooke Smith delivered the speech, and I sat bolt upright.

From then on I was in a state of nearly sick excitement, nervous sweat oozing out of me. But I also happened to know, having once studied *Uncle Vanya,* that Sonya gives the last speech in the play, a curtain speech, and for various reasons I was afraid of it. And when we finally got there, to that speech, I found myself first disabled with tears, and then very close to sobs. The movie ended and I could not leave the theater. I had to be ushered out by the pimply teenaged usher, who took a very dim view of me. "Show's over, man," he said, broom in hand. I drove back home, thinking, "What just happened?"

2. *Tears*

To paraphrase Stephen Dobyns's poem "Lil' Darlin'," *I don't like tears.* And not just because I'm a man. I don't believe in tears because the feelings behind them often have force but also no content; often, if there *is* content, the content is unreliable. Tears are an unstable and unseemly aesthetic response; they are a sign of intensity but not necessarily of quality or precision. Good art is always precise. Just because a reaction is intense doesn't mean that it's true, or accurate. Tears suggest manipulation in the aesthetic materials, or a personal vulnerability to certain kinds of subject matter. A one-time friend of mine who had a mild sociopathic streak once observed to me that people cry at movies and books not because what they had seen or read was true but *because they had been exposed to something they wished were true but that they knew to be false.* That is, the untruth (*not* the truth) of something causes you to cry.

This is a good reason not to believe in tears. These considerations also deposit us in the dreaded land of Sentimentality, where we don't know where we are. More of this later.

3. *What Sonya Says—(a quick paraphrase)*

At the end of *Uncle Vanya,* Sonya has discovered that Dr. Astrov, with whom she is in love, will never love her in return. Astrov is, instead, attracted to Sonya's beautiful stepmother, Elena, who eventually rejects him. Sonya's uncle Vanya has also fallen in love with Elena, who finds Vanya ridiculous. Elena, in turn, is unhappily married to someone I will refer to simply as "the professor," a pretentious hypochondriac who has schemes to sell off the estate but who is blocked in these efforts by Vanya and Sonya, who actually own it. There are other characters. By the end of the play, Sonya has been grievously disappointed in love and in life. Vanya's disappointments are similar and equally intense. In the last act, out of love and desperation, she has been compelled to talk her beloved uncle out of suicide. Then the beautiful stepmother, the professor, and Dr. Astrov depart in their respective sleighs, leaving Sonya alone with her uncle and a couple of other minor characters.

Chekhov has a purely dramatic problem here, which is that every one of his central characters, including Astrov, has been disappointed or frustrated or abandoned. If the curtain were to close on this situation, the playwright would have a truthful but unsatisfyingly undramatic finale on his hands. It would be like trying to end a story in which all the characters have lost everything. Chekhov did write such stories. Nevertheless, he usually avoided endings of that type, where the events may seem to be true to life, but within the story, do not *feel* right. "In the Ravine" is a bit like that. Aesthetic excitement should always trump depressive feelings. So Sonya's final speech provides the play with a grand and desperate rhetorical flourish that is uplifting, or is meant to be, a big moment in which happiness and sorrow, the past and the present, are combined (Eugene O'Neill does the same thing at the end of *Long Day's Journey into Night*—and most of Shakespeare's plays end with this kind of curtain speech, as does *The Great Gatsby*).

Depending on which translation from the Russian you use, Sonya makes approximately three assertions in her curtain speech.

1. She and her uncle will go on working without reward, and then they'll die ("meekly" or "submissively" or "without complaining" depending on the translation).
2. In the afterlife she and her uncle will tell God their story, and they will look down on the world and life, now made "beautiful" and "bright," and they will reflect back on their sufferings with peace and forbearance.
3. She and her uncle will be at peace (or will "rest") and their sufferings will be transformed into a caress; for the two of them, an absence of joy in life will turn, after death, into

repose. In effect, they will experience redemption. *I believe this,* Sonya insists; *I really do.*

4. *Charlie Is Suspicious*

But there is something wrong, off-key, that makes me suspicious in retrospect about this speech's content: Sonya has rarely in the play mentioned God or faith or the afterlife or religion or angels. She is, as one of my students once said, an "earthy girl." All this leaves the suspicion dawning in the mind that Sonya doesn't actually believe a word of what she's saying. There's another small detail in the speech that makes the observer skeptical: Sonya says that she believes all this, and then she repeats that phrase, in a protesting-too-much style: *yes, yes, she really believes it, she really does.* She asserts her belief several times. She insists on it. Who wouldn't be skeptical? She's formulating these claims about redemption to cheer up her uncle Vanya, and maybe to cheer up herself, and to cheer up an unwary audience sitting out there in the dark. In effect, she's double-voicing: She's saying what she would like to be true as if it *were* true, even though she probably knows it isn't. In speaking to her uncle, Sonya is really talking to herself. That's the nature of double-voicing. People talk to themselves when they are ostensibly talking to others, and they talk themselves this way out of despair all the time. These rhetorical maneuvers don't get into literature that often, or, rather, they do, and we don't bother to notice.

5. *A Note on the Translations (from Valerie Laken, my former student and a fine fiction writer in her own right)*

"In general Chekhov translations are not too suspect, mainly because he doesn't play with language too much, not as much as most other big Russian authors. But a couple of points that just occurred to me off the bat: his language feels a bit simpler than some translations I've seen. For example, the Ronald Hingley translation I have has the line, 'We shall hear the angels, we shall see the sky sparkling with diamonds.' Well, this feels slightly flowery to me. There is no 'sparkling' in the original (it's just 'We will see the whole sky in diamonds'). There is no shall/will difference in Russian. And there are no articles in Russian either, no 'the' or 'a/an,' so, for example, that line could also be translated as 'We will hear angels' (not 'the' angels, which to me assumes they exist). Minor matters, surely, but to me Sonya doesn't seem like a flowery girl but a more practical one. One other quick note: the last word, 'otdokhnem,' the phrase that keeps getting repeated, which in Hingley is translated as 'we shall find peace.' What he's rendering as 'to find peace' is really one Russian verb, 'otdokhnut.' It certainly does mean 'to find peace,' but interestingly it is much more commonly used to mean 'to rest, to relax, to rest up, to take a vacation.' It is the everyday go-to verb for any of those meanings, a very common (not lofty) verb. So anyway, it obviously resonates with all the work Sonya and Vanya are doing in that scene and in general."

6. *One Translator, Laurence Senelick, Is Also Suspicious*

"The Russian, *My otdokhnyom,* connotes 'We shall breathe easily' and is connected etymologically to words such as *dushno,* used by characters to say they are being stifled. The literal English translation, 'We shall rest,' with its harsh dental ending, fails to convey Sonya's meaning sonically or spiritually."

7. *Peace, Rest. What's the Difference?*

The reason this matters so much is that we can't really be sure what Sonya means "spiritually" or otherwise in this speech. In a way, there is no literal meaning; it's all metaphoric. She has given us no spiritual context for her remarks. She is speaking about a

hypothetical condition. She's improvising a solution. And what
she is offering up in this hypothesis is a quasi-Christian explanation for the logic of life's suffering. It's not heaven she's offering to her uncle, exactly; it's rest. It's ordinary: a kind of plain
old catnap that goes on for eternity. Of course, sometimes sleep
looks like heaven, especially if you're an insomniac, as both
Vanya and Sonya are in the play (the play is full of insomniacs).

Most versions of heaven are, I am compelled to say, implausible. The story of heaven is not a story that I happen to believe,
unless heaven is also here and now and within. But "rest" is
not particularly implausible, and both words imply the other:
Peace involves rest, most of the time, and rest is nearly always
peaceful.

8. *Charlie Is Still Suspicious*

But no matter how you parse Sonya's last speech, no matter
how you translate it, there is still life beyond the grave; there
is still a god who listens rather than speaks and who does not
condemn; there are still angels, and diamonds; there is still a
flood of mercy (or "compassion that will fill the world"). And
all these artifacts of faith are appearing in the play for the first
time, like props brought on from the wings by busy stagehands
in the play's closing moments. Rhetoric is the deus ex machina
here, and Sonya is insisting on it, insisting three times that she
believes what she says. Within this desperate and fevered set of
assertions, there is also, almost literally, a god and an afterlife
brought on in the machine to be on the stage to save the situation, and the play, and Vanya, and maybe Sonya, too, as well as
the ticket holders. But if God and the angels are the solution,
then what is the problem?

The problem in the closing pages of *Uncle Vanya* is the problem the entire play has created, which is the problem of living

without hope, the problem of depression and of despair that follows suffering. *Uncle Vanya* is very clearly about a particular theme, which is not true of all of Chekhov's plays. But *Uncle Vanya* is consistently about spiritual, sexual, and career disappointment: having a set of hopes and then seeing them dashed. In life such problems must be solved one way or another and put into a place where the disappointment is somehow endurable, and the threat of despair or depression does not loom ominously. The subject matter in turn creates an aesthetic problem—that is, how to present suffering so that the object that holds it (the play, the story) is aesthetically satisfying. This problem invariably leads to a second challenge, which requires an answer of some sort: How does one go on living in a condition of despair? How do you continue if you've been fatally disappointed by your life? If your life has failed, if your hopes have failed, if nothing has worked out, if you've been disappointed in everything you've tried, if you cannot imagine a future, then why go on living? Don't say, "masochism." That's no answer. In *The Myth of Sisyphus*, Albert Camus famously observed, "There is but one truly philosophical problem, and that is suicide. Judging whether life is or is not worth living amounts to answering the fundamental question of philosophy."

How do you deal with depression and despair in a play or a story or a poem without making the play or the story or the poem depressing and aesthetically unsatisfying? Or sentimental and sententious? Is this a pseudoproblem? I don't think so.

Despair, at the close of *Uncle Vanya,* is Sonya's challenge. Aesthetic deflation—flatness—is Chekhov's. Sonya's task is to remedy a murderous melancholia, to address that question, and to solve Chekhov's problem into the bargain: Because she loves her uncle Vanya, she must cheer him up enough so that he (and she herself) can live. Chekhov must write a speech that will give the play the appearance if not the reality of uplift. Sonya is not thinking of herself, but of course she can't avoid considering her own situation as a spinster-to-be, and by speaking to Vanya, perhaps she will cheer herself up as well. How she does this should be of interest to any writer or to anyone who has wrestled with this particular beast.

What happens is that Sonya gets carried away. She knows it, Vanya knows it, but often, I think, the audience doesn't know it.

Sonya begins by telling Vanya to wait. Waiting is what one does when all the alternatives are dire, impossible, or closed off. Then, because she really can't see any earthly solution, she says something she probably doesn't believe about *the* or *an* afterlife, and because the weight of despair is finally too much for anyone to bear, there comes a moment when she herself is swept away by what she is saying and begins to believe it herself. Double-voicing occurs when *a need overcomes skepticism or even common sense;* and faith, or a comforting hypothesis, is poured in to fill that void. This is heartbreaking to witness. The speaker, who begins by improvising, starts to believe his or her own words, and then insists on that belief. In parallel situations, the salesman begins to believe his own pitch; the liar loses track of his lies. Sonya, as I've suggested, is speaking to Vanya but really she addresses herself. And after all, her situation mirrors his.

Chekhov is always asking us this question, "How does anyone live with emptiness?" His stories and plays often create a condition bordering on despair, in which happiness is located elsewhere, such as Moscow for the three sisters, or in loving Dr. Astrov for Sonya, or the preservation of the countryside for Dr. Astrov himself. And then, when no expectation finds its way into actuality, Chekhov's plays grandly, and heroically, struggle with their aftermath condition, and characters begin telling each other what they themselves need to hear. No one is better than Chekhov in depicting the conversations of people shut out from Heaven.

It is not quite right to say that double-voicing appears whenever we are trying to explain and to will a wish into existence—I mean, when we are trying to engineer wish fulfillment. Double-voicing can appear at any time when I'm trying to say something to you and you serve as my means to speak to myself publically about my condition. The content could be a wish, or it could be anything that the "I" needs to hear. I may or may not realize that I'm talking to myself; dramatically, it hardly matters.

Near the end of Paula Fox's novel *Desperate Characters,* for example, Otto says to Sophie, his wife, "I wish someone would tell me how I can live." Otto and Sophie's summer house has been vandalized, and they are standing in the middle of the wreckage in the living room. Otto thinks they should move.

"How about Halifax?" [Otto asks]
"It's only furniture . . ." [Sophie says]
"There isn't any place for the way I feel."
"Listen, Otto. *It was just furniture.*" [Sophie is talking to herself; she'd stay calmer if she weren't.]

There follows a dialogue that, point for point, all but doubles for the concluding moves in Chekhov's play in its strategies for coping with violence and emptiness. Paula Fox's novels, and Fyodor Dostoyevsky's, and André Malraux's (and Saul Bellow's) are interfused with such moments.

Really, you can find double-voicings everywhere. It's not hard to write them yourself if you're aware of what your characters are doing, and particularly if they themselves are unaware of it. I'm describing the land of rationalizations, and rationalizations are always, by nature, dramatic. In its meanest and cruelest form, double-voicing occurs when the bullshitter gets carried away by his own bullshit and starts to believe it. (This is not, I hasten to add, the situation with Sonya, who is not trying to profit from her uncle or to take advantage of him.) Double-voicing can be found in pristine, mint condition in many of Ernest Hemingway's stories, with his blankly stoic characters reassuring their timid inner selves by heartily and manfully reassuring others. Note the schizophrenia in this situation, a schizophrenia that I have always felt is endemic to Hemingway's fiction. In Hemingway, double-voicing comes very close to a cosmological constant. Instead of being about God or rest or the angels, the statements are about enduring in the face of things, or getting over those things. "There isn't any good in promising," Nick says, at the conclusion of "Cross-Country Snow," letting himself off the hook that marriage and his wife's pregnancy have hung him on.

The dying man, surrounded by attendants, says, "Hey. I'm all right." Who is he talking to, if not himself?

9. Sentimental? Sentimental How?

Thus, by a circuitous route, we are back at the problem of sentimentality; Hemingway, as some have argued, presents a form of masculinist sentimentality, while Chekhov . . . well, Chekhov does something else. The question of what sentimentality is, is actually a tricky one to ask, because in fact nobody really knows what sentimentality is anymore.

Nevertheless, whenever I talk to my friend, The Cold Fish, about *Uncle Vanya*, The Cold Fish always tells me that the ending is sentimental, which is why, he claims, my eyes spurt tears.

"Sentimental" was not always defined this way. In the nineteenth century every educated person knew that "sentimental" was the adjectival modifier derived from "sentiment," as in the German poet Friedrich Schiller's famous essay "On the Naive and Sentimental in Literature" (*Über naive und sentimental-ische Dichtung,* 1795). As the composer John Adams has written, "The 'unconscious' artists are the *naive* ones. For them art is a natural form of expression, uncompromised by self-analysis or worry over its place in the historical continuum." The sentimental artist, by contrast, being self-aware, tries to find the lost unity of the naive; he is essentially a searcher, all too aware of his place in history.

By these definitions, every student enrolled in an M.F.A. program is a sentimental artist. I do not mean this as a literary or existentialist critique. We are all latecomers in the history of literature, and most of us agree that pure spontaneity is lost to us, and that we must learn the forms if we are to succeed at what we want to do.

In the nineteenth century, the sentiments consisted of the entire keyboard of our feelings. Every key on the keyboard sounded a different sentiment. Our task as human beings (were we to live in that era as literate citizens) would be to educate our sentiments, to learn and perhaps master our emotions by feeling our way through adolescence and young adulthood, the usual trial and error, learning to play this particular keyboard. We would learn the tonalities of our emotions and how they are played, but *not* in an effort to get rid of them. It is arguable whether our feelings can be mastered, but in the nineteenth century many people thought that they could be. *The Blue Flower* by Penelope Fitzgerald is a wonderful introduction to these ideas. Gustave Flaubert's novel *Sentimental Education,* which Robert Baldick has called "undoubtedly the most influential French novel of the nineteenth century, and to many minds the greatest," concerns the coming-of-age and learning-through-disillusion of its protagonist, Frédéric. Frédéric's education of his sentiments hasn't been maudlin and has nothing to do with maudlin displays of emotion; that connotation is missing from the word's use in that period. "Sentimental" used as a term of negative critique arose later, as a reaction to the onslaught of sensibility and the mostly inaccurate rhetoric of pure feeling. Feeling cannot analyze itself simply by using the language of feeling. But for Flaubert and for his contemporaries, even in English, "sentimental" simply referred to the keyboard, not to the rhetoric.

10. *The Inexistence of Insentimentality*

In our century, following the First World War, the word "sentimental" gradually grew to mean "manipulatively maudlin." Sentimentality was understood to be a form of extremity. In retrospect, the word was attached to certain texts, such as Charles Dickens's *The Old Curiosity Shop,* and to certain scenes, such as the death of Little Nell in that novel. Dickens's *A Christmas Carol* is a touchstone of the sentimental, with its hilariously angelic cripple, Tiny Tim, crying out, "God bless us, every one," and its extremist villain, the hideous Ebenezer Scrooge, converted in one night from mean-spirited penny-pincher to openhearted benefactor. Sentimentality, understood this way, is rhetorical, that is, always going for the tear ducts, trying to accomplish with emotion what it cannot manage any other way. It traffics in stories of innocence versus villainy and is the first cousin of melodrama. There is something fascist about sentimentality, even when it is used for populist or progressivist ends. It wants you to feel and not to think. It avoids thought by invoking emotion, and only emotion, instead. All its ideas exist simply to evoke an emotion, typically of tears, or rage. John Irving, for example, is a great admirer of the art of *A Christmas Carol,* and you can see him deploying many of its tropes at the end of *The Cider House Rules.*

So I am arguing that manipulative aesthetic effects certainly exist, but that there is something deeply mistaken about the use of the word "sentimental" in contemporary writing workshops and in contemporary criticism generally. The word should be temporarily banned. It's close to being meaningless. We don't know what we're talking about when we use this word now because it points to an extreme for which there is no other corresponding point in the spectrum. It's as if we tried to define "day" without having any word for "night." We know what "day" is because we know what "night" is. But if a work is "sentimental," then what quality stands over there as its opposite? "Unsentimental"? What is that? It's praise. But what is any aesthetic object that lacks feeling and emotion and sentiment? The game is rigged: We don't have a word for that condition. John Gardner suggested "frigid," but I have never heard anyone use that word in any context in over twenty years of workshopping fiction, and I have heard people use the word "sentimental" more often than I've had hot dinners.

11. *Back to Sonya*

Uncle Vanya cannot be considered a sentimental *play* simply because of Sonya's last speech. If anything is sentimental, it is the speech itself (or maybe Sonya is, by saying it), but the closer one looks at the speech—its habit on insisting on what is most dubious, its double-voicing, its desperate invocation to God and the angels and a belief in the afterlife—it begins to look more and more like a symptom rather than a statement. In the film version, Wallace Shawn, as Vanya, laughs twice during the speech, as if he realizes how preposterous Sonya's words are, and he shakes his head as if to indicate that—no, he doesn't believe it. Even Sonya, in this version, laughs at herself, at her own symptoms. Chekhov, after all, was a doctor, and often his characters act and speak in what I'd call a symptomatic way. It is as if Chekhov were saying, "Look. This is what people say and do when they're in despair. Don't blame me if this is what Sonya says. It's beautiful, in a way, and besides, almost everyone talks like this or thinks like this sooner or later. All I'm doing is reporting on what someone says in the depths of this particular condition. That's my task."

It isn't as if Sonya is asking for the moon and the stars. Her hopes are small. Her last words are, "We'll be at peace." This is sentimental?

12. *Another Theory of Tears*

I don't believe what Sonya says but I want to, even if it's untrue. Like Shawn's Vanya, I laugh at her, at first, and I shake my head. And then, when I'm confronted by a hope for peace—this minimal hope, this ordinary wish, this humble carrot held out in front of me—I can't stand it, and my defenses give way.

13. *Spin-offs*

What's also interesting about Sonya's last speech is how it seems to have resonated with poets and memoirists. It is explicitly referred to in Donald Justice's last poem, "There is a gold light in certain old paintings." This poem is the final one in his *Collected Poems,* from 2004, published by Knopf. Of its three stanzas, the first evokes the imagery of Christianity and its afterlife, the second, Greek mythology (and *its* afterlife). The third stanza remembers Sonya's last speech, though now shorn of God and therefore entirely secularized. Sonya is given the last word, and the last words of Donald Justice's entire poetic career. Justice's stanzas here have very soft cadences, and end-line word repetitions on the second and fourth lines and the two concluding lines of each stanza. Word repetitions of this sort, at least from Tennyson's "Ulysses" onward, typically convey a sense of weariness, resignation and inaction, though not, I think, of harmony.

"There is a gold light in certain old paintings"

1

There is a gold light in certain old paintings
That represents a diffusion of sunlight.
It is like happiness, when we are happy.
It comes from everywhere and from nowhere at once, this light,
  And the poor soldiers sprawled at the foot of the cross
  Share in its charity equally with the cross.

2

Orpheus hesitated beside the black river.
With so much to look forward to he looked back.
We think he sang then, but the song is lost.
At least he had seen once more the beloved back.
  I say the song went this way: *O prolong*
  Now the sorrow if that is all there is to prolong.

3

The world is very dusty, uncle. Let us work.
One day the sickness shall pass from the earth for good.
The orchard will bloom; someone will play the guitar.
Our work will be seen as strong and clean and good.
  And all that we suffered through having existed
  Shall be forgotten as though it had never existed.

We find Sonya's last speech also evoked in Peter Trachtenberg's brilliant *7 Tattoos: A Memoir in the Flesh,* from 1997, a meditation on the author's vices and self-abuses, and that ends with a coda in which Trachtenberg announces himself as a convert to Sonya's set of beliefs, of quietude and baseline minimal hopes.

14. *The Man with the Blue Guitar*

Chekhov specifies in his stage directions that Sonya's last speech
is accompanied from its halfway point onward by the music of
a guitar, played by Telegin, a bit of an oaf, but a nice oaf. In the
movie, this music is omitted, as is Sonya's insistence on her own
belief and her observation that her uncle is weeping.

When you are pouring your guts out, someone is almost
always off in the next room, practicing the accordion or cut-
ting coupons out of the newspaper or vacuuming up the bread
crumbs under the dining-room table. Icarus falls out of the sky,
and the farmer goes on plowing his fields. Someone is not paying attention, and Chekhov always notices this: how the world
is ending in one room, and in the other room, people are playing cards and getting drunk or playing the guitar. I understand
that Telegin's music may be a consolation, but I don't hear it
that way.

In Charles Ives's great piece *The Unanswered Question*, the
trumpet keeps asking the same musical question, getting more
and more frenzied and desperate, and underneath the trumpet, the orchestra just goes on playing the same cycle of major
chords, like the universe slowly circling around itself, ignoring
its own agony.

15. *Wallace Shawn's Shake of the Head*

In the movie version of Sonya's last speech, Wally Shawn, as
Vanya, at a critical moment, shakes his head and laughs. He
doesn't believe what Sonya is telling him, either. He doesn't believe any of it. Christianity is offering up its meager portion of
comfort once again. But he listens. He can't move. Even Sonya
laughs once, at the preposterousness of what she's saying.

When someone is trying to console you—"things will get
better, you'll get well, the world will be interesting again, look at

how much better you feel"—the temptation is always to laugh, to disbelieve. And yet you sit there, and listen.

In the stage directions, Vanya is crying. Wallace Shawn's shake of the head amounts to a similar refusal of comfort.

That shake of the head says, "No, none of this is true. You know it, and I know it."

And yet, in despair, you do not move. You stay because what you are listening to is the noise of consolation, detached from its utility. "Keep talking, J.P.," the narrator of Raymond Carver's "Where I'm Calling From" says. In his condition, he says, he'd listen to someone who was talking about how he took up playing horseshoes.

16. *Sonya's Last Speech*

In the film by Louis Malle, the director holds Vanya and Sonya, doubles for each other, in a two-shot, Vanya in profile and Sonya full in the face, so that we see them both onscreen at the same time. Sonya is subtly backlit so that her hair has a halo-like glow.

Now, in the early years of the twenty-first century, is there any consolation left to us for the horrors we have witnessed (even by proxy) and the various despairs, depressions, and traumas we have suffered? Is comfort possible to us, in any form at all, in an epoch of holocausts? Comfort and consolation may, indeed, have passed from our lives; it is just possible that we are, historically, beyond them. This is not a trivial matter. To reformulate an old Marxist sentence, *Tell me what you think of Sonya's last speech, and I will tell you who and what you are.*

Note

"There is a gold light in certain old paintings," from *Collected Poems* by Donald Justice, copyright © 2004 by Donald Justice. Used by permission of Alfred A. Knopf, a division of Random House, Inc.

Charles Baxter was born in Minneapolis and graduated from Macalester College, in Saint Paul. After completing graduate work in English at the State University of New York at Buffalo, he taught for several years at Wayne State University in Detroit. In 1989, he moved to the Department of English at the University of Michigan–Ann Arbor and its MFA program. He now teaches at the University of Minnesota.

Baxter is the author of twelve books, including most recently *Gryphon: New and Selected Stories*. He is the editor of *The Art of* series, and the author of *The Art of Subtext: Beyond Plot*.

The text of *Burning Down the House* is set in Minion Pro, an original typeface designed by Robert Slimbach in 1990. Book design by Ann Sudmeier. Composition by BookMobile Design and Publishing Services, Minneapolis, Minnesota. Manufactured by Versa Press on acid-free paper.